CELEBRITY AUTHORS' SECRETS

The World's Greatest Living Authors Reveal How They Sell Millions of Books

STEPHANIE J. HALE

www.CelebrityAuthorsSecrets.com

Copyright

Powerhouse Publications
94/124 London Road,
Oxford
OX3 9FN

Print Edition

British Library Cataloguing in Publication Data.
A catalogue record for this book is available from the British Library.

For Cormac, Tierni and Chiara –
the best Muses anyone could wish for.

Reviews

"You'll learn priority insider secrets directly from the mouths of the world's most successful authors in publishing history and uncover what it really took them to seriously make it huge in the publishing arena.

"Their revelations were so astonishing, I refused to put this book down – and I can say this from my experience of either broadcasting or appearing on every major news outlet on the planet over the past 25 years."

Marie O'Riordan
Award-Winning Film Maker
www.TheForeverMethod.com

"Stephanie has created an exceptional and very useful book for anyone interested in becoming a bestselling author. Being an international bestselling author myself, I still learned A LOT from this book!

"I appreciate the insider techniques, knowledge and real-life experiences shared, and have no doubt that this will be the 'go to' guide for many authors."

Ewen Chia
#1 International Bestselling Author of
How I Made My First Million on the Internet and How You Can Too!
www.InternetMillionaires.com

"These celebrity authors were once unknown and filled with self-doubt. This is a must-have guide for all writers whether self-published or traditionally published. Revealing and inspiring!"

Dr. Joe Vitale
Author of *The Attractor Factor*
Star of the hit movie 'The Secret'
www.MrFire.com

4

"In this book, Stephanie details priceless information and secrets from authors who have collectively sold 800 million books.

"This book provides easy-to-follow tips and strategies, and outlines exactly where to get the biggest results, and importantly how to avoid the pitfalls and disappointing promotion strategies.

"This book is not only fact-filled and easy to read but also a must-read for every author, whether mainstream or self-published."

Selva Sugunendran
#1 Bestselling Author and 'Success through Wellness' Coach
www.MakeAFortuneInTheWellnessIndustry.com

"If you think bestsellers happen by chance, think again. Twelve of the world's most well-known authors reveal how they sell millions and millions of books. And bestsellerdom isn't as random as you might think! Celebrity Authors' Secrets *offers valuable insights into what you should be doing if you want to sell more books."*

Peter Thomson
Peter Thomson International plc
www.PeterThomson.com

"Authors now have a great opportunity to learn from those who have blazed the trail before them with Stephanie Hale's new book. If you are looking for proven strategies to be one of the rare successful bestselling authors in the world, study every word of this masterpiece."

Peggy McColl
New York Times Bestselling Author
www.PeggyMcColl.com

"This book proves what I have suspected all along – that being a bestselling author of millions of books doesn't happen by chance. It happens as the result of discipline, passion and the right mindset.

"Stephanie Hale reveals the patterns in the behaviour of legendary authors of our times – showing both the similarities and the differences in the way they write and promote their books and attract new readers."

Marcus de Maria
International Wealth Trainer and Investor
www.investment-mastery.com

Contents

STEPHANIE J. HALE

"It takes just 12 seconds to decide whether to buy a book."

Stephanie J. Hale is founder of Oxford Literary Consultancy and the Millionaire Bootcamp for Authors.

She is a former Assistant Director of Creative Writing at the University of Oxford, and a former literature adviser to the Arts Council of England.

She is a publishing expert who has been helping authors to write, launch, and promote their books for over 20 years.

"How do I sell more copies of my book?" This is the question I get asked more often than any other.

Over the years, my clients have included: authors with Hollywood and television adaptations of their books; Man Booker judges and Whitbread Prize winners; 'guru' authors who are at the top of their fields; bestselling authors who have already sold hundreds of thousands of books. Yet they ask me this same question with as much passion as new authors who are writing books for the first time.

So who better to share this secret than some of the most successful authors alive in the world today. Collectively, these authors have sold a staggering number of books – more than 800 million copies in total. Nor are these one-hit wonders. These authors have gone on to write one bestselling book after another, after another, after another.

As you read on, remember that each of these writers was once unknown and unheard of, rejected by agents and publishers, or filled with self-doubt. For example, John Gray's ground-breaking book, *Men Are from Mars, Women Are from Venus*, was initially rejected by more than ten publishers who didn't like the title. James Redfield travelled around America giving away 1,500 copies of his book *The Celestine Prophecy* in order to kick-start sales. Eric Carle's much-loved children's classic *The Very Hungry Caterpillar* was originally conceived as a seemingly unmarketable story about a worm that ate holes through pages. It is rare indeed for an author to effortlessly achieve overnight success – however it might seem once the publicity machine swings into action.

So what exactly is the difference between an 'average' book and a book that sells tens of millions or hundreds of millions of copies? How did these authors make their books stand out from all the others? How did they become such international icons? What are they doing that other writers aren't and what can we learn from them?

As you may have guessed already, writing a book that sells millions of copies isn't just about glamour and fame. It's about darned hard work. So I've scratched beneath the surface to reveal the practicalities of what it *really* means day to day.

You'll discover valuable insights such as:

- How many words should you write each day?
- Which rituals will help you keep on track while you're writing?
- What is the best way to plot a book?
- Which criticisms should you take on board and which should you ignore?
- What should you write about on your blog, or on Facebook or Twitter to attract new readers?
- Which forms of book promotion are most powerful and which are a waste of time?
- How to get the audience to buy more books when you speak at events and literary festivals.
- How to keep journalists focused on positives rather than negatives.
- How to cope with unpleasant book reviews, both online and offline.
- How do e-book sales compare with those of paperbacks or hardbacks?
- Will a pseudonym allow you more freedom to write?
- Plus much more.

We're all aware that publishing has changed. What you may not realise is exactly *how much* it's changed. The digital revolution has completely overturned the old system and brought in a brand-new set of 'rules'. The tricks that helped to sell books yesterday are no longer as effective today. No one can afford to ignore these momentous changes – whether you're writing your first book or you're already an established author.

Astonishingly, less than 100 UK and US authors have sold more than a million copies of a single book since Nielsen BookScan started keeping records in 1998. Yet in spite of their extraordinary success, their attitude is less "I know it all" than "I need to know more." There is certainly no such thing as resting on their laurels.

During my time at Oxford University, teaching creative writing and literature to some of the world's brightest minds, we would mentally separate students into those with 'open shutters' and those with 'closed shutters'. Students with 'closed shutters' hated having their work criticised, were resistant to change, and tended to stay stuck in their ways. Those with 'open shutters' loved being criticised, embraced change, and more often than not outshone their peers.

To extend the same metaphor, the authors in this book don't just have their shutters wide open, but their windows and doors too! All of them are avid, if not voracious, readers. All of them are acutely aware of the changes brought about by the new digital age. Even the most technophobic have developed Internet skills and an online presence. In short, they are committed to pushing themselves ever forwards, to refining their skills, and staying ahead of their game.

Although they're some of the busiest people on the planet, they've set aside time to share their knowledge, such as:

- How to test out book ideas on social media to find out what readers are likely to enjoy most and what they're likely to hate.
- Why it pays to safeguard e-book rights in the small print of agents' and publishers' contracts.
- Why tweeting, blogging and Facebook posts may be a better use of time than giving a reading in a bookstore or a library.
- How to deal with the new breed of 'negative fans' who take sport in reading books they hate, then posting vicious reviews on Amazon, Goodreads and elsewhere.
- How to use Twitter, Facebook and blogs to attract new readers and lucrative partnership deals.
- What to do to combat 'showrooming', which happens when readers seek out the cheapest book prices online via their mobile phones. This can be devastating to your book sales if you're not careful.

It takes a reader around 12 seconds to decide whether or not to buy a book. That's the amount of time you have to convince them with your book title, your cover design, and your synopsis. So what is it these authors know that others don't? How did they break through from anonymity to literary stardom? How have they sustained their popularity? How have they managed to write one bestselling book after another?

You'll find the answers you're seeking here in this book. All that's left is for you to keep your shutters wide open, stay receptive to new ideas, and take the necessary action. For more helpful publishing tips, please sign up at: www.CelebrityAuthorsSecrets.com.

Here's to shining your own light on the world, and to selling more copies of your books than you ever dreamed possible.

JEFFREY ARCHER

"I once did a signing session … where four people turned up."

Jeffrey Archer is the only author to have had a number-one bestseller in fiction (15 times), short stories (four times), *and* non-fiction (*The Prison Diaries*).

A former politician, and deputy chairman of the Conservative Party, he established himself as a literary force with the publication of his first novel, *Not a Penny More, Not a Penny Less*, in 1975.

Since then, his international book sales have passed 270 million copies: he has been published in 97 countries and in more than 37 languages.

He is currently working on a seven-part series of novels titled *The Clifton Chronicles*.

I didn't start writing until I was 34 years old, almost by mistake. But I didn't realise I was a storyteller and that this in itself is a God-given gift – much as playing the piano, being an opera singer, or being a ballet dancer is. It's a gift. I didn't realise I had it until I left the House of Commons at the age of 34 and couldn't get a job and wrote my first book, *Not a Penny More, Not a Penny Less.*

You say you stumbled upon it. Many successful authors speak about their early impulse to be a storyteller or a writer, which over the years increasingly becomes a business. They talk about the 'business' of being an author. Do you see it as a business?

No, I certainly do not. I'm a storyteller. I tell stories and if people are kind enough to read them, I consider myself very lucky. I don't deny that it has made me a fortune, but that isn't what drives me now. I haven't needed money in that sense for many, many years, and that isn't what drives me. I want *The Clifton Chronicles* to be the best thing I've ever done.

You're quite disciplined, aren't you, in your approach to writing?

The word "quite" is irrelevant! I am *totally* disciplined. I rise at about 5:30 am; work from 6:00 to 8:00; take a two-hour break; work from 10:00 to 12:00; take a two-hour break; work from 2:00 to 4:00; take a two-hour break; work from 6:00 to 8:00; go to bed about 9:30 or 10:00; and get up again at 5:30. I can't flat-out concentrate for more than two hours. My wife can do four or five hours. I get a break when I take a walk or have a meal or watch a film or something, and I'm ready to go back, all guns firing. So two hours is flat-out for me.

Do you set yourself a writing target each day?

No. It pretty well ends up the same anyway; it ends up at 1,500 to 2,000 words a day, but I don't set the target because I'm concentrating on the story.

You don't plan your books do you?

No planning at all: I haven't got a blooming clue! I pray a lot. [*Laughs*]

Do you have any rituals or is there anything that particularly helps you? Do you meditate or anything similar?

I rest for 20 minutes before going into a writing session. I lie flat on the bed, rest, probably going through the chapter and thinking it through, so that my brain is absolutely on the book. So when I walk across to my writing room, I'm in the right frame of mind. It's bad to have just had a discussion with someone or just done something, and then go straight in. I like those 20 minutes to compose myself.

Where do you draw inspiration? Is it mainly from your life and people you meet?

I think I've been lucky in having a very interesting life and meeting lots of interesting people. But I'm bound to say Jane Austen managed it in a small village, writing about her mother desperately trying to get rid of daughters. She wrote six novels, and every one of them was a bestseller. In the end, you've got to be a storyteller. It doesn't matter how interesting or varied your life is. If you can't tell a story, then you're not in the game.

Would you say you still enjoy writing? Do you still feel excited by it?

Assuming I've got a story to tell, I love it. I always have so far. If a story is bubbling, I absolutely *love* it.

What do you find most challenging about writing?

Well, I think it's the sheer hard work, the sheer discipline. To young people who say, "I've written a book," I say, "I doubt it; you've probably written a first draft!" My books have had 13 or 14 drafts, every one of them handwritten. So, it's hard work and it's a marathon every time. You've got to accept that it's a marathon, and if you're not willing to, well ...

People imagine they can knock out something in a weekend and it's going to go to number one and they're going to be world-famous the week after. They can think again, because it takes a lot of hard work. There are exceptions to the rule. Of course there are, but they're once in a lifetime or once every 20 years.

Publishing has changed enormously over the duration of your career as a writer, as a result of the Internet and e-books and Kindle books.

It certainly has!

Do you think these changes are a good thing and do you embrace them?

Do I think it's a good thing? I think it means the demise of bookshops and of hardback books. That's a bad thing. Do I embrace it? You'd be bloody stupid not to! Five years ago, I'd say 5 percent of my sales were on e-books; it's now 50 percent. I'd be mad not to embrace it! I was checking my figures on my Kindle right before speaking to you.

Do you keep a regular check on your sales figures?
You better believe it. I'm fascinated by how many people read me.

How regularly do you check things like your sales figures?

The sales figures, once a week – because the only way you can get them is through your publisher. But you can check on Kindle how many people are reading you by your reviews. It's a pretty vague way of doing it, but it's not that stupid. If you check your Kindle, you'll see 500 people have made comments on *Sins of a Father*, 400 on *Only Time Will Tell*, and just under 400 on my latest book. They've done just under 400 in six weeks! There are only two or three authors in the world getting those figures. So it's a quick way of checking.

How much do you use social media to promote your books? You use a lot of videos on YouTube, don't you?

I have YouTube and then I have a Facebook page and I do a blog. Last month it hit 3.5 million people. And I have Twitter! I tweeted this morning that I went to the Roy Lichtenstein exhibition at the Tate Modern, so I'm telling them something every day.

It can be quite time-consuming, can't it, social media? Which is your preferred social media?

Well, you say that, but I spend half an hour a day on it, no more. I'm not willing to become a devotee where I'm sending out something every three minutes. I can't be into that. No, I do one tweet a day, sometimes two, or sometimes none. I do a blog every two or three days, and Facebook takes care of itself.

Do you think this is a good way to keep in touch with your readers?
It's a very good way. It's ironic that they've now proved to me that I'm better off doing that than doing a tour of the United States.

Wow. Can you expand on that?

Well, in the days of *Kane and Abel*, which sold 37 million copies, I did 17 cities in 21 days. I was a young man, but I was exhausted at the end of it.

They don't bother to send me to New York now. They say, "Put a blog out, put a tweet out, Jeffrey. Let everybody know it's coming," and my fans read the blogs or the tweets or Facebook, so they know it's coming. If I go to San Francisco, 150 or 200 people come out for a signing session. It's not worth it!

Do you have any tips for using social media? Do you tweet about things that you do in your day or do you tweet about contents of your books? What is most effective?

Yesterday I went to the launch of the Margaret Thatcher book at Banqueting House, so that was something to tell people about. This morning I went to the Roy Lichtenstein exhibition. I'm lunching at a theatre club today. I'm doing a charity auction tonight. It's non-stop, really, I just tell them what I'm doing. Except when I'm writing, of course, then I just go into hibernation and write.

How much time do you spend promoting your books, as opposed to writing your books? Or do you see it all as one and the same thing?

No, I don't. I would say 5 percent promoting. Mind you, how can you tell? If someone calls up and says, "We'd like you to come and talk to us about Margaret Thatcher," I don't mention the books, but there I am on television or whatever it is. Do you call that promotion or is that just part of my life? Tricky question – but if you're saying *direct* promotion, it's 5 percent.

You've been described as one of the greatest storytellers of all time. If you had to identify the key ingredients that make up a great story, what would you say they are?

You have to have a beginning, middle and an end, and you have to make sure people have to turn the page. When they get to the end of a chapter, they have to curse you. I love it when people write and say, "I sat up all night. I got to the end of the chapter and thought, 'Damn you.'" That's great! That's what I'm trying to achieve.

What sort of things do you do to make them turn the pages?

You can't answer that question: there is no answer. What does a ballet dancer do? What does a pianist do? What does a singer do? I don't know! It's a God-given gift.

What would you say, then, to aspiring writers?

You just used the word again: *writer*! That's the difference, you see. The great Dadie Rylands, an emeritus professor at Cambridge, said for every thousand writers, there was one storyteller. Storytellers are a very rare breed. A *thousand* books are sent to publishers every week, as you well know! They get a thousand books a week, the poor things. There probably is a storyteller in there somewhere, but they can't read the thousand books.

Who are the writers – or storytellers – who most inspire you?

Oh, you're getting better! [*Laughs*]. I love Dumas, Dickens, and the short storyteller writers: H.H. Munro (Saki) and Maupassant, an Indian writer called R.K. Narayan. I think he's wonderful. I love reading a story. Of course I love Jane Austen. I love anybody who can make me turn the page.

Do you spend much time reading? Do you have the time?

I am non-stop reading. I was up at 6:00 this morning reading. The next book's got a lot of banking in it, so I'm reading a lot of banking books at the moment. In the fifth of *The Clifton Chronicles*, Sebastian is going to be a banker and I'm just picking up as much knowledge as I can. On the sheer pleasure side, yes, I read a lot of novels.

Do you keep notes? Do you keep a notebook or anything like that to jot down ideas?

Nope. Just pop it in the brain, and leave it there if it isn't good enough. I leave it there and let it percolate.

So you're a great believer that if it's important, it'll stick?

It'll percolate too. It'll run around in your mind and go in a different direction. It'll siphon off this way, it'll disappear, and it'll come back … You never know when it's going to come in a book, what sentence or something that happens, some experience. You may never know, but then suddenly it'll appear!

Which comes first, the title or the book?

Every time that's different. *Kane and Abel* was very late. I was walking down the Embankment in London, and it was at that time called *The Protagonists*, and then it was called *The Brothers*. It was all sorts of names and then suddenly *Kane and Abel* came, and I knew immediately. In fact, I rushed back to find out if anyone had ever used it. I was terrified that someone else might have used *Kane and Abel*. So titles just come. The next book title came before I started writing. The last one came after I'd finished. It varies greatly.

Do you think your book title is important to sales?

It's not important if you're already established. But I spend a lot of time on titles and I really care about them. If you look at *The Clifton Chronicles*, some people think *Only Time Will Tell* is the best title I've ever had. For a saga, it tells you everything: it's going to be long, it's going to take time, and we're not going to get there. Generally thinking, *Not a Penny More, Not a Penny Less* has always been a popular title. I work hard on them.

You mentioned before that virtual tours or blogging or tweeting are more effective than offline book tours.

That's what the publishers say.

Which do you prefer?

In person. When I to go to India (which is madness of course) I love it. They mob you and 3,000 people come to hear you speak. It's weird.

So you enjoy the face-to-face contact?

The answer to that, again just answering you bluntly, is if four people turned up, you wouldn't. But I recently spoke in Dubai and 700 people got into the room, so they held another meeting the next night and another 700 got in. The answer is: if they turn up, it's wonderful; if they don't, it's pretty blooming boring. I once did a signing session maybe 20 years ago in Holland where four people turned up. That was a long trip for four people!

If you started your writing career over again, is there anything you'd do differently?

No. You can only learn from experience. You can only become a better craftsman. You're a storyteller from day one. There are still a percentage of my fans who think *Not a Penny More, Not a Penny Less* is the best book I've ever written. I'm a much better craftsman nowadays. I'm much better at the technique, but that's only years and years of doing it. The storytelling I don't think has improved. I think if you're a storyteller, you're a storyteller.

How would you say your technique has developed and changed over the years? Do you think your stories have become more sophisticated?

Yes, I have a better command of language. I think you get better; it's like anything. If you're a banker, or a doctor, or even a surgeon, your first operation is your first operation.

But if you're doing it ten years later and you're top of your profession, you're probably going to be better at it. That doesn't mean the gift that God has given you to operate on people has improved, you've just got a better technique. You have a better use of time, too. When you write your first book, you haven't got a clue how long it's going to take or how to go about it. You get better and better at it. It's like marathon running, really. Once you've done a few, you begin to know that it's 26 miles and how long it'll take, and where it'll be painful, etc., etc.

You do lots of media interviews, don't you? How do you cope with all the interest from the media: can you offer any suggestions and helpful tips for other authors? Do you prepare beforehand?

No, you don't, because you can't know what the questions are and you can't know where they're coming from. You're better not to, in my experience. You're better to go on and face it head on.

Obviously if it's a subject like Margaret Thatcher or it's a subject like your book or whatever the subject is, you have mental sentences prepared, of course you do, but you may not be able to get them in. You can't tell where they're coming from or what they're interviewing you about. Margaret Thatcher interviews were particularly tricky in that way because you could never be sure of the angle they would be coming from. That's the fascinating thing, though; you learn to live off your wits.

That's interesting. John Gray, the author of *Men Are from Mars*, says he always prepares what he's going to say beforehand, no matter what questions he's asked.

Well, that's what politicians normally do and of course he's right. He wants to get certain points over. I make sure I want to get certain points over, of course I do, but they get very bored with you if you do that. If they think you're a good interview and you've been interesting, they're much more likely to ring you up and say, "We'd like you on again, please, Jeffrey." But if you just say, "MY BOOK IS CALLED *BEST KEPT SECRET*. IT'S BEEN NUMBER ONE ALL OVER THE WORLD. IT SOLD 27 MILLION COPIES. YOU SHOULD GO AND BUY IT," they won't invite you again.

Are media interviews still effective in driving your book sales?

Oh yes, unquestionably. The biggest problem an established author has is letting people know the book is there. I had a Member of Parliament say to me the other day, "Are you still writing, Jeffrey?" The last ten books have been number one, and he's asking if I'm still writing! I didn't get cross, but what it taught me was there are thousands, millions of people out there who not only have never heard of you, but don't even know you write! The answer to your question is: yes, any opportunity you get to let people know you're there, or to let people know you're a writer, is a bonus.

Can you share a little bit about the book you're writing at the moment?

Do you mean the fourth in *The Clifton Chronicles*, or the one that's currently at number one?

The fourth in *The Clifton Chronicles* – the one that you're actually writing.

No I cannot, you wicked woman! When does your book come out?

I'm not sure yet.

Ah, I'd better be careful then … Hold on, I'm going to seek advice … *[Break in the interview]* I'll give you the title of the next one, but please don't tell anyone else before it's launched; it's *Be Careful What You Wish For*.

Nice title.

I agree, but don't tell anyone! That'll be number four, and I have a major problem. I had originally promised to write five in *The Clifton Chronicles*, and I got to the end of four, and Harry Clifton, the hero of *The Clifton Chronicles* is only 44! So at some point I'm going to start telling the world, though I've started semi-telling them, there's more likely to be seven books than five.

I can't get him from 44 to 80 in one book! I can't do it! I've been caught there by myself – I actually set out telling my publisher and the world that I was going to cover 100 years in five books. I've so far covered 44 years in four books. So I'm not doing very well!

I'm sure your readers will be absolutely delighted!

I hope so. The second book was the Second World War, 1939 to 1945. I couldn't then, getting to the end of the war, suddenly say, "Well, I'm now going to give you another 150 pages." I couldn't do it; I really came to a natural end.

Have you thought beyond your *Chronicles*?

Yes, I'll be doing a set of 12 short stories. Then I'm finally going to write a book that I've wanted to write for many, many years, and that I think will be the toughest challenge I've ever had in my life. That will take at least a couple of years.

What is that book about – are you allowed to say?

That's fiction, and no, I am not telling you anything about it at all!

Is that because it's going to be the toughest emotionally or because of the research involved?

The research will be quite tough, but the idea, the concept, is probably the best idea I've ever had in my life. It's been sitting in the back of my mind now for five years, and by the time I get to it, it's going to be one hell of a challenge.

ANNE RICE

"It's a wonderful time for books – like no time in history."

Anne Rice is best known for her bestselling series of novels, *The Vampire Chronicles*. These books resulted in the Oscar-nominated film adaptation *Interview with the Vampire* starring Tom Cruise, Brad Pitt and Kirsten Dunst.

She has also authored erotic fiction under the pen names Anne Rampling and A.N. Roquelaure.

Her books have sold over 100 million copies. At the height of her popularity in the 1990s, it was estimated one of her books was sold every 24 seconds.

I always dreamed of becoming a writer. It was a recurring dream all through childhood, and I did a lot of writing when I was a child. I'd break off and quit for a few years, and then I'd go back to it. It was always what I wanted to do.

I remember trying to write a story when I couldn't even spell anything, and I had to ask my grandmother or my mother to spell every word.

Do you still have any copies of those original stories?

No, not a thing! Everything is lost. I've often wished that we were a family that saved such things. My father did save one little story that I did when I was about 12. He did save that and now that is buried in storage somewhere, but I wrote much longer stories in notebooks that have been lost.

During the 1990s, one of your books was being sold every 24 seconds! How did you feel at that time?

That was a very intense period. I think I was enjoying life very much. But when you succeed and you fulfil your dreams, you also inherit a sudden intensity that can make it very blindingly difficult for you to experience every moment. So much is happening that you have a sense of things getting by you on all sides, and there can even be a desire to retreat, to shut down and to go into exile. But it was wonderful.

When you sit down to write a book, do you still feel excited about writing? Or do you have to push through some kind of pain barrier?

Well, certainly in the beginning of any book, there is a pain barrier to push through. You put it very well; that's what it's like. It can take me months to really get going into a book, but once it starts to roll, there's no joy in the world that's any greater than writing a book. It's just wonderful to wake up every morning and think, 'I have to get in there and find out what's going to happen next!' It's just tremendous, but for me, that only happens after a certain point.

There's a lot of time spent trying to break inside of a book. There's dreaming and research and planning and scheming, and then comes a time when I have to stop all that and really start writing. It is very difficult, and there are many false starts and a kind of obsessive-compulsive going back to the beginning. I have to get through all of that and it can be very difficult. With some books it's harder than others.

Tell me a little about your writing process. What does your writing day look like? Do you have a rigid schedule or is it more fluid than that?

It becomes pretty rigid, but it's very convenient. I live here in a small house, very far away from everything. I don't have a social calendar; it doesn't exist. I just do exactly as I please. What I really love to do is get up in the morning, go eat something, and then go write. Then I just break for lunch at exactly the same time every day, and then go back and write. Then after dinner, I usually write for about two hours more. I usually quit by eight o'clock. I eat the meals regularly because I'm a diabetic. It's very simple. I have to eat at exactly one o'clock and exactly at five o'clock. It really makes things easy as a writer. Again, I don't go out; I don't go places. When I'm working on a book, I can just devote my whole time to it.

Then when I finish a book, there will be a period where I will go out and see people, have dinner with friends, and maybe travel a short trip somewhere, but then I get back to my working routine. But that's how I like to do it when I'm writing. The best time for me is probably the afternoon and the early evening. I can't stay up all night any more. I get physically sick if I stay up all night.

So you used to stay up all night in the early days, but that's had to change?

Oh yeah, I've written whole books totally at night! Even recently, I wrote them at night to get away from all distractions, but I can't do it any more. I get very sick from that kind of upset schedule, and I guess my body is just too old to do it.

Do you prefer total silence or music in the background when you're writing?

No, I can't write with music or have any distraction at all. It upsets my rhythm. I have to *hear* the sentences as I'm writing them. I'm sitting at the computer pretty much whispering them out loud or hearing them in my head, and I can't write to music. I think writing to music can be very bad. You might think your writing is wonderful because you have this stormy music soundtrack, and then you turn it off and read your writing and it can be very thin.

Do you set yourself a word count for each day? Or are you just happy with whatever you get done?

I don't set a word count. I pretty much write through an incident, like I want to get through one big incident or one development in the book. It's very comfortable for me to do about 15 to 20 pages a day, and also to go back over the whole manuscript and bring it up to the present state. The computer makes it so easy. It was never that easy when we just worked on typewriters. Now you can go back and go over the pages and pick up little inconsistencies and bring everything up to agreement with what you're doing. I like to roll forward 15 or 20 pages, but it's not always that easy. That's when it's rolling.

Do you plan your books out first, and if so, to what degree? Do you have a series of bullet points, or is it quite detailed?

I think it varies from book to book, but it works best for me when there's not so much planning. When it gets over-planned and over-imagined, then it's harder than ever to get into it, because you've got so much of a vision of what it *should* be, and every time you start it, you fall short of that vision. But, the longer I go on, not breaking in there and not getting going, the more I do plan and envision. The thing about planning is it can help tremendously to have a vague idea of the end and the middle. It can help a lot, but you have to be ready to scrap that plan. You have to be ready to let the story flow in some new or surprising way and throw that plan out totally if that's what you have to do.

Do you have any rituals that help you while you're writing?

I like to have coffee right there, and I like to have Diet Coke right there. I have a carafe of coffee right by my keyboard, and I drink out of a demitasse cup so it will always be hot. I keep pouring, and drinking from this little cup, like shots of hot coffee. I also like to have the Diet Coke. I find that anything that keeps you from getting up from the keyboard, that keeps you right at it, is good. The coffee, the Diet Coke, maybe even chewing gum, so that you don't get up and feel the need to take a break. I like that very much.

I have an exercise cycle in my office so that if I get stiff, I walk about three steps and get on it and pedal to wake my legs up. It's a very nice small office. It's hard to move in it, but in a way, it's perfect. I have a window to the street and I can see people out there walking their dogs. It's very peaceful. I live in the California desert away from Los Angeles, on this little gated street and it's very pleasant. I can see the olive tree outside and the grass, and people walking their dogs. That's almost all you see in this little community. We're not an open street. We're like a closed little gated area. So I love it.

When your work goes off to your publisher nowadays, how much influence do you have on things like the covers of your books?

I've been with the same team now for over 30 years. I'm with Knopf in the United States and Random House in the UK. I have almost no input on the covers. I mean, usually they show me the cover when they're finished, and I say, "Wonderful!" I approve of it. I have very little input. I can pretty much vote down a cover if I really am disappointed or confused, and I have done that, but I don't have much input into what they actually offer me. Even when I vote one down, they'll come back with another one and it's going to be their idea. My editor, Vicky Wilson, has done some stunningly wonderful covers on my books. So I really have a lot of trust in her to come up with some great things. I think the covers in the UK have been fabulous, but they're very different from the ones in America, and I don't even try to guess why. As I said, I don't have much input really in the creation of the covers.

How easy do you find it to come up with titles for your books?

I come up with the titles through a very long, emotional process, and I usually have the title before I begin the book. I almost have to have the title. It can change, but I have to have it. No one has ever pressured me to change a title. Though they did with my recent book, *The Wolves of Midwinter*. The original title was *Yuletide at Nideck Point*. We found we were dealing with a generation of people that don't know the meaning of Yuletide, so we changed it to *The Wolves of Midwinter*. But I've never had anyone pressure me to change it against my will.

The name of the house is Nideck Point, and that title confused people because first, they don't know what Yuletide is, and second of all, they don't know what Nideck Point is until they get into the book and know the name of the house. I guess it would be like *Winter at Mandalay* – if you know what Mandalay is, it makes sense, but if you don't ... So anyway, we did change it. I was very surprised that the up-and-coming generation doesn't know what Yule or Yuletide is. I was very surprised, but I understand this is going out to the public, and anyway *The Wolves of Midwinter* is fine.

That brings me neatly to my next question ... Which criticism do you listen to and which do you ignore? How much attention do you pay to critics?

Every writer has to decide how to do that. It gets down to what makes you write and what makes you not write. I myself like to read every review at least once. I do check Amazon and I read all of the reviews written on all of my titles at least once. But if you find that that's blocking you and you can't write, that's one indication that you shouldn't listen to it. If it makes you feel like slitting your wrists or never going to your keyboard again, that may be an indication that you shouldn't read it. If you feel excited even at a negative review, and you think, 'Oh yes, I see that' or 'I know what to do about that. Let me go back and think about that,' then that's an indication that you should listen to it. But I think it's a very painful and difficult thing.

I think most writers have been through such a process of trial and error by the time a book sees print, that they've been over all the different possibilities in their mind. It's pretty much a finished product for them; it's the best they can do! A lot of criticism that you get is really just beside the point. It's like somebody criticising *A Christmas Carol* for being around Christmas – it is what it is. You have to get a pretty thick skin to ignore the inappropriate criticism. I think that is a real problem today. Years ago, before the Internet, there were always painful, negative reviews. You would read them and they would be painful. They could crush you or you could sometimes ignore them and think, 'Well okay, I see the point but I don't regret what I did,' or you could even learn something from them and think, 'Okay, that's fair, so let me think about that in my next book.'

Today on the Internet there's so much inappropriate criticism that I think it can be very destructive to a writer and very hurtful, and I understand why a lot of writers don't read it. Most of the writers I know don't go to Amazon. They won't. I understand, but I've been writing now for over 35 years. I'm not sure when I was younger that I could've taken it, the constant inappropriate reviews. They're criticising Hemingway for not being Faulkner, or Faulkner for not being Tolstoy, or Tolstoy for not being Hemingway, and it goes on and on and on. We have such a body of that criticism online now as part of the public record that it can be hurtful to a writer. At the same time, it's wonderful for books that they stay alive for 30 years on the Internet. People can go on now and write a review for a book that was published five years, ten years, 30 years, or 100 years ago! So it's a wonderful time for books – like no time in history. Books stay alive now on the Internet and Amazon and Barnes & Noble and other sites. It's incredible. The good far outweighs the bad. But when it comes to criticism, writers are facing a mountain of criticism that they didn't face in the past.

I think you know what helps you and what builds your enthusiasm to write, and I do believe a negative review can do that. You can read it and think, 'Yeah, that's true. I can see why that reader was disappointed and I understand that,' and you can be emboldened to go and do better on your next novel. There are a lot of things that can be good about it, but I see a lot of pain when I look at this world that writers live in today. I see a lot of pain on the Internet and I'm not sure what the solution is.

On your website, you post questions for your readers and you give answers to your readers. You obviously seem to enjoy the interaction – having feedback and having an opportunity to respond. Is that interaction always a positive thing?

It works out very well for me on the Facebook page. The readers are really pretty wonderful on that page. I couldn't do it if they made specific suggestions. You know, if they said, "Have the hero or the wolf go to India!" [*Laughs*] That would block me completely, but people just don't do that. What they generally do is give you an idea of what they really enjoyed, or when they're negative what they didn't enjoy. Frankly, I love talking to them about these things. I will ask them questions. I'll say, "When you look at my books and say this is the one you like best, can you tell me why? What was it that it gave you?" and they've given me a lot of insights into how it all works. I just love interacting with them every day.

How much time do you spend on social media every day? You have a Facebook and Twitter account, don't you? Do you use anything else?

No. But everything I post on Facebook is automatically going to Twitter. I very seldom actually tweet anything, other than via Facebook. I don't spend that much time though, you'd be amazed. Over and over, I'll break during my writing and flash over there to Facebook and see what's going on. I'll read a lot of comments very rapidly, and I'll put up a new post and I will get into the discussions, but I can do that in maybe 20 minutes and then go back to work. There are some times when we get into involved discussions on politics or art, music, whatever, that I will stay on the page maybe 45 minutes talking with people, arguing with people, and reading what they have to say about something. I enjoy that, but it's not as much time as you would think. Because it's all happening on one computer, it's very easy to go back to writing or back to my research and then take a quick Facebook break.

So do you see that as a way of keeping in touch with readers or testing your ideas on readers? How do you view social media?

I think, for me, it's a marvellous opportunity to communicate with them very directly, to answer their questions very specifically, to ask them questions and to get these priceless gems of feedback from them. I love it!

I can ask them almost anything, even for recommendations. I'll say, "I saw this fabulous movie. Do you have any recommendations for others like this?" and they will! I've got an enormous number of recommendations from them for musicians and singers, violinists, actors and motion pictures that I never would have stumbled upon on my own. That's fabulous. When I'm writing a book, I don't really tip my hand to what I'm actually writing. I don't ask them specifically about it, but I'll ask them general things. Now they're coming on the page and saying that they're reading *The Wolf Gift* and they remember when I talked about this or that topic and they see it in the text. That's kind of fun and interesting. But I never tip my hand of what I'm actually doing. I never post work in progress or run an idea by them. I couldn't do that. I have to develop it all in my soul. I can ask them any number of general questions. What did you like least about *The Witching Hour*? What did you like the most? What characters stood out to you? It's really from all this very positive feedback that I've learned a lot of things.

How do sales of your physical books compare to e-books these days?

It's changing rapidly. On my last novel, the last I heard, they were 50 percent. For every 100 hardcovers, they were selling maybe 50 e-books. So the total for e-books was half of the final total for hardcovers. So that's amazing, because it was not that way in the past, but e-books are gaining popularity every week. My readers in particular like hardcovers. They're kind of known for that, they're collectors. My books in paperback don't do that well. It's in hardcover that they do well because these readers tend to like hardcovers. I'm that kind of person myself; I prefer hardcover to any other form. We post about e-books too – we talk about this a lot online – and I ask my readers what they think about it. All the time, you see more and more people recommending e-books. In the beginning, it was a minority. Now they're *all* admitting that they're going to e-books for various reasons.

I don't know what the future is going to hold. I think as soon as Amazon, or some entity like Amazon, can create a hardcover-on-demand the way they can now create a paperback-on-demand, that is going to be a very tough moment for conventional publishing. Unless conventional publishing moves toward creating hardcovers-on-demand instead of warehousing and shipping – that's what is killing them, warehousing and shipping. They're going to have to start developing some sort of technological centre in a bookstore that can print a book up for you right there and bind it. It's entirely conceivable; it's already being done in paperback. So as soon as they can do that with quality paper and fonts and beautiful covers, it's going to be over for the old model.

Many authors are moving more towards online book promotion rather than traditional offline book tours. Is this the same for you?

Well, I'm getting the same demand as usual to go on tour. The problem is the bookstores aren't there any more. I'm getting a lot of requests to come sign in this place or that place, a lot of requests to meet people individually in an autograph line. I think that will continue but the problem is, the bookstores where we used to go over the years – to have these wonderful big signings – they don't exist any more. They're dying out. They're closing. They're gone!

I've talked a lot with my publisher about this and they tell me that system is just not there any more. I know we are planning a tour soon and we will be going to bookstores in a number of cities all over the country, but it's nothing like in the past. There just aren't that many. I do think the time will come when authors will do signings probably from some central place like a hotel ballroom or conference room, and people will buy their books online and come to that ballroom to meet the author and get a signature. The reason I say a hotel ballroom is because that works very well. You can have *hors d'oeuvres* and a bar there, and you can have chairs for people to sit in, and you can have a big table where you can sit and meet the people as they line up. I've done that in certain places. When it's been done in the past, you usually have a bookstore bringing books to the site. But now, as bookstores die out and you have whole cities and towns where there is no bookstore, I think it's going to be that kind of signing. It's going to be a signing of the future where you do advertise it online and you tell everybody, "Get your books online and I will be there from 8 pm to 10 pm on Monday night at this hotel in the ballroom and we will have refreshments for you." I love that. I totally love meeting them. It may never be like it was in the past with eight-hour signings, but a two-and-a-half-hour signing is a lot of fun for me and so I look forward to that.

I read somewhere that at one point you had to limit your signings to a thousand people in order to keep from getting cramps in your hand. Is that right?

No, I never limited it. I just went on signing as long as I could. I made it a challenge that I would be there until the last person came through. Sometimes the bookstores end up limiting it, they say "we're just not going to get through these people" and then they just want me to simply autograph and not sign their names for them. That's a terrible thing when that happens because the people who've been standing there the longest don't get their names in the books, they only get mine. We try to avoid that. I've signed for eight hours straight at a number of places, a number of times. Not in recent years. Social media has really changed that. People don't come to bookstores in the same numbers any more to meet each other the way they did at those old signings. They're meeting on Facebook and in clubs and online. We definitely did signings that went on for incredible numbers. We've never limited to any number deliberately, not that I know of.

Do you think that the Internet has changed the way in which readers read?

I don't think so. No, I don't believe that it has. I think if you look at the novels that are selling today, they're not that different from the novels of the past. If you take a *Jack Reacher* novel, a thriller by Lee Child, something very popular, it's moving a lot like Dashiell Hammett or Raymond Chandler in the past, maybe a little faster, but not a whole lot. There are differences in style. But I don't see that much of a change, and there are novelists today writing huge big thick books that go on and on, like the *Game of Thrones* books by George Martin. They're wonderful. It is true that they move fairly fast, but they're taking their time to tell their story, they really are, and they're using a lot of characters very much the way the older books did. I mean nobody today is going to take the time that Tolstoy took. But on the other hand, I'm not so sure that's true. There may be somebody out there writing who's the next Tolstoy. People are producing huge books today. I think genuine readers look for a variety of types of experience, and that has not changed over the years. The one thing I know my readers want is they prefer the bigger books to the shorter books. They want more story, they want more depth. They do not appreciate it when I experiment with a more hardboiled or stripped-down style. They tend to prefer my more verbose style. They've let me know that, but I still like to experiment and do different types of books in different ways. So no, I don't see a lot of change.

I see that reviewing problem that I've talked about. Where some people sadly have discovered that they can enjoy tearing a series apart as much as they enjoy reading it. You have what's called the "negative reader". I believe a writer called Laurell K. Hamilton called them that, the "negative reader". It's the rise of the negative fan. You have these people who will read book after book of an author who they say they hate and they will go into great detail of why they hate this book compared to all the others. You see, we never had that in the past! If somebody didn't like your book, they didn't read it. They do this on the Internet and they enjoy it. It's like a game to them. It's a way of enjoying the author and the series that we didn't see before. If you want to see it, go to Charlaine Harris or her last book *Dead Ever After*, and see what the negative fans have done on the Amazon site for the book. It's just unbelievable. They no-vote every positive review. It's like a game. The author has become like a video game, and you can play that game negatively or positively. I think that it's just as much fun for them to kick someone in the teeth as it is to say, "I enjoy your work." I have people like this, but they're in the minority, thank heaven. I have a few who come on all the time and say, "Well, her last six books have been horrible and this one's worse." You really want to say, "Why are you reading it? What's wrong with you? Has somebody got you locked in a room with a gun to your head? Don't read the books if you think they're so bad!" [*Laughs*] I have a few who do this all the time. They enjoy going into long litanies of what they hate about the book and why it's just terrible and so forth.

Other than the phenomenon of the negative fan and the inappropriate criticism, I wouldn't say the Internet has changed readers much. Genuine people who enjoy books, they still want to read a good story. People in publishing speculate over it changing and they think maybe it's best to change over to short books, but not readers. I've never heard any reader yet who wanted to read short books. They may enjoy a short book now and then, like *The Bridges of Madison County* or something, and it may be wonderful, but that's not what they want. When you look into the statistics, it turns out that the longer books are the ones that sell a lot. It's just something I've learned over the years because they put a lot of pressure on you not to write a long book. They don't mean to, they just can't help themselves. They're always pressuring you not to write, but the readers love it. They love it when Stephen King comes out with a huge book like *The Stand*. They love it. It gives them a longer experience, and that's what they want.

You've written under two pseudonyms in addition to Anne Rice. Have you ever felt like creating another pseudonym and writing something completely different, because you have the freedom to write with anonymity?

Yes, I have. I've thought of it again, but I don't think I'll do it. I have so many books right now that I want to do just as Anne Rice that I don't think I'll ever get to it. Every now and then I think of writing more erotica under yet another pseudonym. But I don't know. It is a wonderful thing to do that – to feel completely private and anonymous and do something totally different. I really did enjoy doing my erotica under the name A.N. Roquelaure, and to see it coming out and being read again today with such interest because of *Fifty Shades of Grey* is wonderful fun.

One piece of advice that you give new writers is that, the world doesn't want someone who sounds like somebody else. The world is crying out for original voices. How do *you* find that original voice?

Gosh, I don't know. I write the book the way I want it to sound. It would be a tragedy if it sounded exactly like someone else. That advice is really for people who are trying to sound like other people. That advice is saying, "Don't knock yourself out trying to sound like Stephen King or Danielle Steel. Sound like yourself. Let *you* speak." Just speak yourself and let all your little problems come to the fore and your own special little traits. Now if you did that and still sounded like someone else, well that'd be a disaster I imagine, but it doesn't usually happen. Usually what happens is some young writers are struggling to always sound like the people they admire and don't trust themselves enough. At some point you get over that and you think, 'I'm just going to go for it no matter how eccentric it is and then see what happens.' We all get criticism telling us that we ought to sound like someone else. I've certainly gotten it.

Well, it's easy to criticise, isn't it? It's a whole lot easier to criticise than it is to go write the book! [*Laughs*] One final question, how do you cope with all the media attention? It must be pretty tough at times feeling under the spotlight, being a celebrity author.

Well, there can be moments that are shocking, but I live pretty quietly without seeing many people. Pretty much, the media spotlight is a choice for me. If someone calls and I don't really want to give a story, I don't. When you go on tour to promote a book, you are grateful for the media attention because it just gets the word out that you have a book! You have a new book and you hope people will want to read it, and then you *hope* the media will give you attention. I very seldom have gotten what I consider to be terribly negative attention from the media. I think actors and actresses and movie people have that problem, but not really authors. We don't have it too much. It can happen, and it does every now and then, but it's not the rule.

ERIC CARLE

"I always write for myself first. I write for the child inside."

Author and illustrator Eric Carle is most famous for *The Very Hungry Caterpillar*, a children's picture book that has been translated into more than 50 languages.

Since it was published in 1969, he has illustrated more than 70 books, most of which he also wrote. More than 100 million copies of his books have been sold around the world.

Eric has won numerous awards for his work and contribution to children's literature.

I feel so fortunate to be able to do the work that I love and to have had so many door openers, so many people in my life who have supported my work: teachers, editors, readers, friends and family.

While I have never received a formal rejection letter from my publishers, I have abandoned book projects on my own. You just start to learn, after a certain number of years, when something isn't true or right.

Also, I have a very wonderful editor, Ann Beneduce, with whom I have worked from the very beginning. Ann has always been supportive, but sometimes she would just 'forget' about a particular project that wasn't right.

You've written over 70 books, and won many awards. If you had to come up with a recipe for a bestselling book, what would the ingredients be? Should authors write with their readers in mind ... or write purely for themselves?

I think that for a book to succeed, it must be well designed. With my own work, my aim is to simplify and refine, be logical and harmonious. Also, I can only say how I do it. I always write for myself first. I write for the child inside.

How important is a book's title to you?

VERY!

Do you plan your books *before* you write them, or do they evolve as you go along?

Yes, once I have the idea for the story, I plan each book out and make many, many thumbnails and dummies to see how the story flows.

But each book also evolves. The hardest part is coming up with the idea. One child wrote to me and asked where ideas come from, then went on to tell me that ideas come from both your outside and your inside. I found that to be a fairly accurate and perceptive assessment.

Did you ever know when you wrote *The Very Hungry Caterpillar* that it would become such a massive success?

Well, for a long time I didn't understand why this book was so popular. My editor and publisher and I asked ourselves, "Why is this book appealing to so many people?" I think its hopeful message: *you too, little caterpillar, can grow up and spread your wings and fly into the wide world*, has struck a chord with many readers. If there's a sense of hope that is taken away from my book, I am very happy.

Did you always dream of being a writer and artist?

I have always loved to draw, ever since I was a child. My father enjoyed drawing and he used to make pictures for me. He would tell me stories while drawing pictures of trees and animals, and sometimes people. Also, my father used to take me on walks in the woods when I was a boy. He'd lift up a rock and show me the small creatures who lived underneath it. I think in my books I honour my father by writing about small living things.

How easy is it for adults to bridge the gap between the adult world and a child's world?

My background is not in the field of education or children's literature or psychology. But I can say that for me, creating books for very young children, who are transitioning from home to school, has been particularly meaningful because that was a difficult transition in my own life. I feel that in a way, my books are attempts to help make this transition easier. I've done this, or attempted to do this, by creating books that have holes in the pages and make sounds; books that you can play with and toys that you can read.

Where do you gain inspiration? Do you ever suffer from writer's block?

Writer's block or any kind of 'creative crisis' is part of being creative; it will never disappear. You have to learn to live with it. I *still* suffer from this 'creative crisis'.

If you started your publishing career again, is there anything you would do differently?

Everything happens in the right time, so "No."

How much of your time do you spend writing your book ... and how much of your time do you spend promoting your books?

I am retired now so I am spending less and less time promoting my work in person. But for years I visited schools and did book signings in bookstores. But now I am enjoying time in my studio and preserving my energy for creative work. But I have made a few video interviews that are designed to simulate the 'in person' visits to my studio.

Do you have any other tips for aspiring artists or published authors?

I often tell people about the four magic letters: DO IT. I want to be encouraging but I can only offer the example of my own experience, which is just one approach. There are many wonderful artists to learn about, which is important. But you must use your own imagination. You have to just do it.

BARBARA TAYLOR BRADFORD

"A novel is a monumental lie that has to have the absolute ring of truth."

Barbara Taylor Bradford, OBE, is the author of *A Woman of Substance*, which ranks as one of the top-ten bestselling novels of all time.

Barbara has written 28 novels – all of which have been bestsellers – and sold more than 89 million copies in over 90 countries. Ten of her books have been made into mini-series and movies for television, produced by her husband, Robert Bradford.

In 1999, Bradford became the first living female author to be featured on a postage stamp, by St Vincent and Grenada.

In 2002, she was again recognised with a postage stamp by the British Isle of Man.

When I'm writing a book, I get up usually at five; sometimes I've been known to get up at four-thirty, but I do get up early. I don't know whether that's just the way I'm made, or the fact that I worked on evening newspapers. I was on the *Yorkshire Evening Post* and I had to be in the office sometimes at seven, and then I was on the *London Evening News* later on, and I had to be in there very early too. But I think it might be the way I'm made. I'm very good early in the morning. I usually sleep well and I get up at five or five-fifteen, sometimes a bit earlier if I'm awake, because there's nothing worse than just lying there waiting for a clock to ring. You might as well get up. So I get up early, I have coffee, something like some Ryvita or toast, and when they come at six o'clock, I look at the British papers that I get. I get a couple of British papers every day, and very quickly glance at them. I don't read them till later in the day: I just like to know what's going on there or what I should know! Then I get dressed in a pair of comfortable trousers and a T-shirt, or a sweater if it's winter, and go to work.

Bob gets up at about seven-thirty-ish, and I then stop what I'm doing and make him two boiled eggs. As soon as he's got his breakfast, I go to work. We say "Good morning", we have a chitchat as I bring him his breakfast and that's it! I'm like Margaret Thatcher in that way, I guess. I have to make sure my husband gets his breakfast before I go to work. So I've often done quite a bit of editing between, let's say, quarter to six and seven-thirty.

I try to always have something to edit from the afternoon before because it kind of gets you back into the routine very quickly. I stop about one-ish and I usually have a salad of something like endive chopped with some tomatoes or maybe a bit of smoked salmon ... I eat a very light lunch, not very much, and go back to work until about four.

That's a long writing day ...

Well, I'm not always writing you see ... Sometimes I'm sitting thinking about plot. I must know the entire book before I can sit down and write myself an outline. I always give the outline to my editor here (in the US) and my editor in London so they know what I'm doing. But I do that outline for myself because I find it very useful as a blueprint, and I try to stick with it. Of course it doesn't always exactly work out that way, but I do try to stick with it.

Do you set yourself a word-count or a target of pages that you have to write? Or does it vary from day to day?

Well, I always try to write between five to seven finished pages. Some days I don't get a lot done because I've thought it out and I've got it down, but it's not right! (I always say to people, "Don't worry if it's not right; you've got something that you can tackle the next day and then get it right.") But normally I do between five and seven finished pages a day. Of course, they do get edited again. I don't have the sort of method that many people do, which is to write a first draft completely. I don't do that and I never have, starting with *A Woman of Substance*. I stay on Chapter One, until I get it as right as I can. I need to keep rewriting and editing till I am satisfied that I've got it the way I want it to be. Then I move on to Chapter Two ... I don't jump around, but if I have an idea or a thought about a character or a scene for later in the book, I do make a separate notation, so I don't forget it or lose it. And that is how I go: Chapter One until it is correct, Chapter Two until it is correct … right to the end of the book. What it means is that when I deliver a book, they are really getting a finished product, because I've done most of the editing myself!

The thing is, I've always broken up my books ... If you look at any of my books, you will see: Part One, Part Two, Part whatever. So once Part One is finished, it's retyped by a typing agency – because as I'm writing, I will send them a completed chapter by fax. It's typed by the agency and put on a disc and they send me back the hard copy. So I've got a hard copy here at my side, and if there are any changes I make them once I've started Part Two.

When Part One is finished, I leave it for a couple of weeks ... then I start writing Part Two, because I think you need space and distance. I think if you're too close to it, immediately when you finish the work, you don't see if there's something wrong. So several weeks later, when I'm working on Part Two, I will take a day and go back and read from page one to let's say page 50 or 100, however long that Part is. I'll see things then, because I have more objectivity; I'm not quite as close because I'm on another segment of the book.

So this is just my way of doing it! I'm very orderly, I'm very disciplined, and I'm very precise. It'll already be retyped by the time I get to the end of a novel. If I'm writing Chapter 30, the typist is typing 29. So I don't have to wait ... I'm getting fed the retyped book while I'm continuing to write. It's kind of a process, which I like because it means when I'm finished and she gets the last chapter, I get it back in a couple days and the book is done. And I've already edited it a great deal.

So usually I get a few notes from both editors on both sides of the Atlantic. They talk to me about it, if they have a comment to make about a change. I believe nothing is written in cement and I think that writers who don't listen to editors are really rather silly! They should! Other eyes should see their work. I don't always agree, and it's my book and my name is on it, as I always point out ... Therefore if there is a criticism, let it be my own mistake and not something they've suggested I do.

But I don't have problems with editors and I never have. I think you do need somebody as a sounding board. You need someone who is there to be able to say, "I love this, but there's too much description" or "You know, a question comes here: could you add a line?" It's that kind of editor. Nobody takes a pencil and slashes the book, because I'm too professional and I always have been, I think maybe because I was a journalist. I get on well with both my editors; I listen to them. Then I pool their advice and sit down with my own clean copy and put all of their suggestions that I'm taking on to that one copy. In other words, if you read the British book and then read the American book, it will be identical.

So do you have any frustrations with your books or characters? People might assume that if you've written as many books as you have, which I believe is 28, that you might not have?

Yes, I'm on my twenty-ninth. You know it's so funny that people think that when you've done it once, it becomes easier. It doesn't! It's just as hard, the second time around as it is the twenty-ninth time around. I think what does happen is that you learn a lot when you've written so many books. You learn ways to cut corners or you learn how to pace the book. Obviously, when you keep doing it over and over again, you learn a technique to do certain things.

I write always about people who are entirely different to any of the ones that have gone before. So of course there are frustrations and you can't always get it right. But I do spend a lot of time thinking out the entire book. A lot of time goes into it daily, before I write that outline. I just looked at the outline the other day. Part of last week and the beginning of this week, I've lost, because of interviews and going out to do some promotions for the publisher here. But normally I'm at it every day. I can go to the outline and say, "Am I missing something? Have I forgotten something?" And there is an outline that could be anything from 15 to 20 pages, which is what I call "extended jacket copy", because as I'm writing it I'm not going into great detail. But that outline helps me and it keeps me on the straight and narrow in a way. But yes, I'm frustrated, and I throw paper away and I struggle with stuff, and sometimes can't get the feeling right that I want to convey. But putting something down on paper is tremendously important, because that way you've got something tomorrow to rewrite. If you've got a blank page tomorrow, then you're staring at a blank page. And that can go on indefinitely if you lose confidence!

So how do you keep up your excitement and enthusiasm when you sit down to write? Are you sometimes bored with it?

Well, I'm bored if I'm not doing it. Bob always says to me, "Why do you still work so hard?" and I say, "Well, because I'm bored when I'm not writing a novel." I get very involved with the characters, and they become very real to me. I believe that that's why they are real to the reader. I think I manage to make them very real on paper. I just enjoy it. It's what I do; it's a way of life. I've done it since I was seven years old!

I started writing in school exercise books. I had a mother who loved books and reading. She taught me to read by the time I was four; when I was five or six, I had my own library cards too. We went to the Upper Armley library, which was this wonderful Victorian building, and she would put me in the children's section and we'd find a couple of books and then I'd take them and look at them. There was a place to sit and read, and she would go hunting for her books. I was writing little stories from a young age, and when I was ten, my mother sent one to a children's magazine. They not only said they would use one of my stories, they paid I think it was seven shillings and six pence – a postal order came – and my destiny was sealed at the age of ten!

Wonderful! And how much of what you write is inspired by personal experience, and how much is outside of your realm? Or is it a blend of the two?

Well, I don't really do research into the characters, because the character comes to me. I sit and think: who is this person; who is this woman that has entered my mind; or who is the man and why are they interesting enough to be written about? A whole book is going to be written about them – why? What are their problems? Where are they going? What motivates them? Those are the sorts of questions I ask myself. I write all that down. You know you've got to have psychological insight into people to be able to be a novelist and I think I'm very strong on that. Once I've developed the characters and a plot, then I know the kind of research that I have to do.

For instance, *Secrets from the Past* is about a woman war photographer, and she came to mind because I suppose I was very surrounded by war in the spring of 2011. I was finishing up a book called *Letter from a Stranger* and war seemed to be all over the place: Afghanistan, Iraq, Kabul, you know that was happening in the news. I'm very much a journalist, so I was listening to all that and I thought, 'I've never written about a woman who was a war photographer.' Almost in that instant, I saw a woman in my mind's eye. I thought, 'Oh! I don't know what she's called, but she is the daughter of a famous war photographer, and she is a war photographer,' and within a week I had that woman wholly developed, and the family, but I didn't really have the story. Then I had to sit down and think out the plot. So I find all this very exciting and very challenging, and that's when I'm doing the research because I've known some war photographers and I've always been a great fan of a man called Robert Capa, who was a very famous war photographer who was killed in Vietnam. He became a celebrity, and at one time had a big love affair with Ingrid Bergman, and he was one of those dashing, charismatic sort of men. So I got all my books out on Robert Capa and just did research on that. Then I needed to know exactly, what were the symptoms of PTSD, because one of the characters comes out of a war with Post-Traumatic Stress Disorder. So it was that kind of research. But before the research comes the idea for the main characters and the protagonist. Then comes the plot: what is this person all about; I have got to tell their story; what is their story? And so then I invent the story, which is actually the drama and the problems, because without drama you don't have any story! Then comes the research to fill in the gaps.

Somebody once said, "How do you explain a novel – after all, it's fiction?" And I said, "Well, it didn't happen, it only happens in the mind of the author." Then, I came up with a line recently, which is that, "A novel is a monumental lie that has to have the absolute ring of truth if it's going to succeed." The ring of truth is the underpinning of the book; it's very genuine, real-life research. I really know how somebody acts if they've got PTSD now; I know what their symptoms are. So it's the research that's the underpinning of this story. For example, there was never an Emma Harte [the heroine of *A Woman of Substance*]. All of these people I've created out of my own head. I suppose that's where the talent lies.

A lot of people think they can be a novelist because they write good prose, but they can't be a novelist if they don't know how to tell a lot of lies. You've got to be able to invent people that didn't exist and don't exist, who do things which have never happened. You've got to have something called an imagination, as well as the ability to write nice prose.

You've got to be able to understand people. You really do have to have insight into what makes people tick, and you've got to able to grab the reader. I remember once I had an editor who said to me, "If you haven't grabbed the reader in the first 50 pages of a book, forget it! They're not going to be interested enough to read on."

So openings are very important?

Yes, I think so. Though it doesn't necessarily have to be something dramatic. For instance, in the book I'm writing now, it begins with a little girl called Cecily walking towards this big house standing on the hill, and she's going to do something there that her mother has asked her to do. Suddenly, a gypsy girl who hangs around the area is in front of her! The girl's in a hurry and she knows this gypsy

– she's seen the girl for a number of years hanging around. Cecily says, "I can't stop to talk to you and I don't have even a ha'penny, so you can't tell my fortune." I can't cross your palm with silver is what she's saying. The gypsy behaves a little oddly, and looks at the house and looks at her, and says, "I know where you're going; you're going up there!" I don't want to tell you too much to give it away. Then the gypsy takes a twig and makes a drawing in the dirt path. Cecily asks what it means, and she says, "Nothing!" She just laughs and skips off over the field. Cecily looks down at it and scrabbles her feet on the little drawing in the dirt and hurries on, thinking, 'Oh she's strange!' It's the mysterious behaviour of the gypsy that will intrigue everybody.

So the opening is not dramatic, it's mysterious. You're thinking, 'what does this mean, these symbols she's put in the dirt, and why is she thinking of the house in a different way?' Then when Cecily gets to the house, the cook, who is fond of her, tells her to go upstairs. As she goes up, the cook thinks, 'I hope she gets away from this place – her aunt didn't.' So there's intrigue created within the first chapter. Why would she want to get away? Why didn't the aunt get away? What is it about this house? What did the gypsy mean? You've a series of things building up in Chapter One. Do you see what I mean? It's not great drama like somebody being shot or having their head chopped off, but it's intrigue and mystery. It's just how I write I guess. You need to engage the reader.

You've learned these tricks and literary devices over time. Is there anything that you would have done differently, if you look back over your career?

Well, my first American editor said to me after reading *A Woman of Substance*, "You're very adjectival, Barbara!" I used a lot of adjectives, which I don't any more. She also looked at me in alarm when I arrived in her office, 30 odd years ago, with two shopping bags. She said to me, "I hope that's two copies!" I said, "No, it's one!" To which she asked, "Well, how long is the book?" and I replied, "One thousand, five hundred and twenty pages and it weighs sixteen and a half pounds." She asked, "How do you know?" I said, "I weighed it at the supermarket!"

So we had a good laugh about that. Then, we cut about 300 to 400 pages, and we lost some minor characters and things like that. But it was my first novel, and I put everything in but the kitchen sink, I suppose, and a lot of adjectives. I have learned to be tighter, and you don't need three adjectives to describe a sky.

Would you say it's been plain sailing for you over the years?

You mean my career? Well, I've always had good publishers who have been good to me. I've been lucky in that sense. I've been with HarperCollins in London for 34 years; they published *A Woman of Substance* in 1979.

I'd better tell you that history, because it's quite interesting! Going back 36 years ago, I was a journalist, but I also wanted to be a novelist ever since that first short story as a child. So I guess in a period of a couple of years I wrote, but did not finish, five novels and they were all in the suspense genre. I realised later that perhaps that wasn't right! Then, one day I literally sat down at my desk and said, "Okay, if you don't write a novel, you're going to one day be very frustrated and wish you'd done it while you were still young! So you must come up with an idea!" Then I asked myself a lot of questions, and I've told people to do this who say they want to be a novelist. I sat with a yellow pad and asked myself what kind of book I wanted to write!

I wrote down: *a traditional family saga*. Then, I went all the way through the questions in my head, supplying an answer to them. Where do you want to set it? Who is it going to be about? At the end, I summed it up: *While reading this list, I see that I want to write about a woman who starts her own business, who becomes successful and wealthy and well-known*, and I actually wrote, *I want to write a book about a woman who becomes a woman of substance*. I then started the next day to wonder, 'All right, when does it start?' And I thought, 'In 1910, when she's a little girl and working in some house as a servant.' I wanted to set it in Yorkshire and I kept referring to my list. I realised that perhaps I should start it in the present, like in the 1960s and then go back to tell the story of this woman. The reason for that was, I thought, 'who wants to read about a little girl scrubbing steps? Why not start it with a woman who's made it, who is probably in her sixties, and we see her success, her power, her influence and how great she is? Then we go back to the past to tell the story of how she became what she is.' And I was proven right about that because I don't think people would want to read about a girl scrubbing floors. Instead, they are like, "Oh, who is this powerful woman?" and she has some setbacks in Part One of the book. What happened was, I did write the outline, about 20 pages, and I showed it to a friend of mine in London who was an agent. He said, "Barbara, this is great! But I hope you write it, because you've had other great ideas that you never finished."

So he mentioned the outline to an editor at Doubleday and she called me. I gave her the outline and I met with her. She said, "Do you have any pages?" and I said, "No, but if you let me know what you think about the outline, I could start writing the first bit of the book and give it to you in a couple of months." She called me the next day and said, "This is the best outline I've read in years and I want to see those pages!" She said, "How about three months' time?" and I said "Fine!" So I gave her 100 pages, and she read them and said, "I'm going to show them to other people here and I'll get back to you in a week." A few days later, she called me and said, "Everybody loves it! We want to make a deal!"

So I work very hard Stephanie, and I'm very diligent; that's a word I would use about myself. There was nothing wrong you see, with those five books I started but didn't finish. But I think it was the actual acceptance by a publisher of my initial 20 pages in the outline that underscored my self-confidence to keep writing. Because I've always had a lot of determination and self-belief, and knowing where I'm going, and what I want and I've gone out after it. I've always been very ambitious and I still am, despite the fact that I've written 28 books. So I think it's a combination of my ability and my character, and who I am. I've had good editors, I've had good publishers, I'm still with HarperCollins – you know I'm their longest standing author. So they have all 28 of my books, and they're waiting now patiently to get the new one.

So it's about who you are as a person; I think character comes into that a lot. I tell people, "I don't sit there eating chocolates, you know. When I'm in that room I'm really working; I'm doing it and you don't do it overnight!"

And you write longhand or with an old-fashioned typewriter, don't you?

Well, it's not old – it's called an IBM Selectric Wheelwriter Number Two. I'm sitting at the desk with a computer looking at me and I research on that, but I'm unable to write on the screen. The weirdest thing – I don't know how to describe it really – I face the screen and something freezes in me! I think I've got to put something on here very quickly, and then I panic. So I don't use the computer for writing, I write in hand. I often start a chapter in hand and then I go to my desk. I'm looking out of the window: at the right side I've got a little table that takes a typewriter, with a lamp on it, and space for the dog underneath. I work on my Wheelwriter Number Two; it has a correcting tape in it. I've had it a few years, but it's not old. I have two actually, in case they stop making them. Then I start typing what I've written in longhand and then I keep going all day on the typewriter. I find longhand great to get myself going.

Do you have any other rituals or routines apart from making Bob his two boiled eggs in the morning?

No, I haven't, I know that I can't. I've been doing some promotion this past week and yesterday. I can't wait for tomorrow because tomorrow I'm going to be able to continue writing the new book, and I'm excited about it. I love to come into this room: it is furnished as a sitting room, but it has a research table, a desk and the typing table, a lot of books I've written and a lot of books for research. I just like being in this room, no other rituals really! I do have the kind of pen that I like to write with, yes – but it's not a Mont Blanc or anything like that – when it runs out of juice, I can get another one easily. I do have a Mont Blanc, but it's not that I use. I like to come in here early in the morning, have my coffee, look at the papers quickly, get dressed, do the work, and I have a rest at the end of the afternoon. Then I have a shower, I put on a Kaftan or trousers and a clean T-shirt if we're staying home, or I get ready if we're going out. I don't accept lunch invitations unless it is a business thing and I have to, or it is somebody's celebration, someone's birthday, because I think it kills the day for me.

I don't think there is any secret except that I'm very disciplined, I rewrite and polish and I try to do my best work all the time. It's a challenge every time! It's like an actress going on the stage – just because she is Judi Dench and has done it for years, doesn't mean that the next movie is going to be easy. Because you're playing a different character, it can be tough. I think we learn tricks and techniques and we understand how to do things faster and better than we did when we were starting. But it's still hard work, and long hours in a chair. I get up and I walk around, I've got a huge apartment, it's far too big but at least I walk around and get a cup of tea or a glass of water, because sitting is terrible, it's bad for you! But I do try to get up and stretch quite a few times and do some walking around. Or I might have to go out to the hairdressers, I usually try to make that around 2 pm or 2.30 pm, so I get a morning's work in. But it's hard work!

How much time do you spend promoting your books? How important do you feel this is? Some authors embrace it and others don't.

Well, I think they're silly if they don't embrace it, especially today. I think it is very tough today for everybody, even if you are a bestselling novelist, because the e-book has ruined the paperback more or less. I'm very big in e-books, thank God! But you know publishing has changed, it's a different business. To tell you the honest truth, I rather enjoy doing the promotion, because you spend a lot of time alone. Somebody once said, "You lead a lonely life," and I said, "No it's not lonely, it's solitary!" I have a solitary occupation; it's not lonely because I've got all these people here in the room with me who really do become very real to me. But look, I'm in this room and it's solitary: I have a dog under here, she's asleep, but it's solitary!

So I'm happy to leave this room and go to England, as I did in February. I did 58 interviews and three events in two weeks, which was non-stop. I had to go up to the BBC in Manchester to be able to do that morning show: *BBC Breakfast*. Then I was in Yorkshire for the *Yorkshire Post* lunch, and an organisation called Welcome to Yorkshire made me an ambassador for Yorkshire. So those were events where I signed books and spoke. That's a lot. However, you get to meet the readers. I think that's very important knowing which books they love. They say things like, "Why did you do it this way?" and "I didn't like that person in the book." So I enjoy it: it gets me out and about, away from the room. That's what I'm saying: if you don't enjoy it, then it's going to be murder to go on the road! I've always thought that if I'm going to do it, I might as well try and enjoy it, because otherwise the person that comes for a book signing will detect it and know that you're not happy doing it. If you're going to do something, you must go out and do it with a good grace!

There have been huge changes in publishing over the last 20 years, and particularly the last ten years. How much online promotion do you do?

A lot! A *lot*! We have someone in my husband's office who does it constantly. My website is constantly added to and changed and updated; and we control the one for England too, the publisher doesn't have to do it. So I have two websites – USA and UK – and I am on Facebook, Twitter and you name it! I have PR people – I give them a lot of stuff and they do it, I don't physically do it myself. I think social networking is very important today.

Yes, social media is one of the fastest ways to reach huge numbers of people. If you go to a book signing or book festival, you're going to reach maybe a thousand people! If you're using online social media, you're reaching hundreds of thousands or even millions of people.

I wrote a piece for my website about Margaret Thatcher recently. I talked about our first meeting and called her a "rock star" and "a woman of substance". That piece was taken by the *Daily Mail* and it went on to the *Daily Mail Online*, which services 110 million people. I'm not saying that 110 million people read my story about Margaret Thatcher, but they glanced at it, and probably glanced at the bottom where it said: "Barbara Taylor Bradford's latest novel is *Secrets from the Past*, HarperCollins," and the price. How can you get to the potential of 110 million people? Then the *Sunday Telegraph* used part of it in a special Margaret Thatcher supplement that they did. They surrounded it with photographs of her and her clothes, because I spoke about how much she loved clothes and handbags and jewellery; she was very feminine in that way. So that blog was used by the *Mail* and the *Sunday Telegraph*, and the *Yorkshire Post* used some of it. Look at the exposure I got with just that!

Fantastic! So how do you feel about the changes in publishing? You sound quite positive about them.

Yes, I think one has to be positive. Well, that's my nature you know, my glass is always half full, not half empty! I think you have to be positive; you have to go out there and do it. I am never going to be defeated, that's not my personality or my character. I've got to always be going forward, moving up, doing it. I am very self-confident and I suppose my mother gave me that. I'm also determined,

I'm driven, I'm ambitious and I still keep going. I don't think that anyone can just sit back and say, "Well, I've written the greatest book that's ever been written!" and hope it sells. I don't care who you are; whether you're John Grisham or Jeffrey Archer or whoever, every author has to do some promotion today. There's so much competition – and not necessarily from other authors – there's competition for a person's free time! What the Internet has done is to take away a lot of people who read books, because now you can read anything you want online: you can research, you can play games, you can download music. It's not just other authors that are taking readers, it's the other options that people have when they want to relax. They don't necessarily have to read a book. I don't just go around thinking, 'I'm competing with other authors.' I'm thinking, 'I've got to get this book out there and get it sold in such a way that people will want to read it instead of downloading iTunes.'

TERRY PRATCHETT

"Writing is a process of breaking yourself and everything you've done into little bits and pasting them on something else."

Photo by Rob Wilkins

Sir Terence ('Terry') Pratchett, OBE, has sold over 85 million books worldwide in 37 languages. He is best known for his comic fantasy novels in the *Discworld* series.

Terry has a penchant for wearing large, black fedora hats, as seen inside the covers of most of his books. In 2001, he won the Carnegie Medal for his children's novel, *The Amazing Maurice and his Educated Rodents*.

His novel *Snuff* sold 55,000 copies within three days of its release and was the third-fastest-selling hardback novel since records began. He has the distinction of being the most shoplifted author in Britain.

We lived in the countryside when I was a child. We played around a bit. I would like to hear books read but I wasn't particularly interested in reading. My mum took a rather commercial attitude about this. On one occasion, she realised that I was falling back and she actually gave me a penny for every page I dictated to her.

So for every page you dictated, you would get a penny?

Yes, when I read out of the book. I thought, 'this was really good' because the pennies were coming in. Then a friend of the family said, "Oh, is he reading? He'll like this." That was *Wind in the Willows*. I've still got the battered old copy here. I was reading that, and that just brought me to life. You have read it I'm sure.

I love that book.

Well, the point is that I was bright enough to know that something weird was going on. We were country people and I knew how big a mole was and how big a badger was and what a toad could do. I knew that these things were talking and acting like Victorian gentlemen and the badger could go down a mole hole. It kind of told me that the world was in flux in a way and you could change it. And you could tell these whopping great lies. [*Laughs*]

My mum didn't have to pay me any more. In fact, I went down to the local library as soon as I could have a ticket. In my very early teens, I spent a lot of time working in the local public library for nothing. I just went and volunteered and did it. That meant I could get my hands on all the books I wanted.

They were just coming out of the time when if you were a child you weren't allowed into the adult library.

Fortuitously, because I now was theoretically a working, day librarian, that meant surely that I was a grown-up. That meant that I could read anything that I wanted to read, even if it was not suitable for me – *especially* if it wasn't suitable for me.

There is a book called *The Child That Books Built* by Francis Spufford. It talks about how books affected him. As soon as I found the library and the joys of reading, that was it. Education didn't really matter. I was doing it all myself.

So writing then was a natural progression from reading?

It seems to have been, yes. I don't quite know what causes that. One thing that I'd like to drop in to the conversation is that a lot of the early stuff that I was reading was science fiction. Fantasy came rather later than that. The thing about science fiction is that if you're quite keen on it, sooner or later, you'll try your hand at doing it as well.

I remember while still at school, I went to my first Science Fiction Convention and then met Arthur C. Clarke and a number of other science fiction writers that you might not have heard of. But Uncle Arthur, you must have heard of him?

Absolutely.

And you could chat with them. These weren't men made of gold, or 40 fathoms, these are real people. In the convention, they would chat to you if you weren't a total dickhead. The science fiction fraternity is very good on that sort of thing. Young up-and-comings get advice and support if necessary.

So when you wrote your very first book, was it easy for you? Or were there any challenges to be overcome along the way?

Well, I regret to I say that I had it incredibly easy. I met a small press publisher, local lad, and this is while I was at that time a young journalist. We're putting a lot of life into a small place here and your readers can find a lot more about me by Googling like mad.

All of the books said that you couldn't really earn a lot of money for life from writing fiction. Everyone sort of knows you can't do that. So I thought, 'I tell you what, if I get the job on the local newspaper at least I'll be paid, and then we can see what happens after that.' Once I found I could do that, I ran away from school in the middle of my A levels. I thought, 'Here's my opportunity. Now I'm a writer. Or at least a journalist!'

But then Colin Smythe, who is the publisher, actually liked my first book, which was a children's book called *The Carpet People*. And there it is. The first one off the stakes and away it went. I feel embarrassed when I hear about other authors' experiences. They say, "It took all those years." And I'm saying, "You know, it was quite easy."

In the process of writing a book, do you plot it before you write it or does it organically evolve?

I think a lot of people will probably say the same thing that I'm going to say now. It's all about your reading. I went through adolescence reading like a combine harvester, reading every single thing. That goes into the back of your brain and it's in there somewhere, and it comes out again when you need it, if you get what I mean.

Yes, I do. Did you take any lessons from being a journalist? Obviously with journalism you're thinking about headlines and you're thinking about the way you're structuring the story.

Well, yes. There are two different types of structuring really. As a young journalist you have to have, "Who's this about and what is it? Why?" You could write down all these different things on a small piece of paper, the things that must be in.

I was a good journalist but I was an even better sub-editor. I spent some time as a sub-editor, and correcting everybody else's writing was what I was really good at. Because I'd read everything: old books, very old books, books from the 1930s. Everything. You don't really know you're doing it, but you're building up knowledge. It springs out when you need to use it. That's the best way I can put it. You don't actually say to yourself, "I'm going to read all this, so I know about *this*." You read this because it's interesting. You pick up bits. Often in a book you're reading, the author will mention something else that you haven't heard of. That drops in.

When I write, these days it's hard to talk about it because I sort of do it automatically. It's hard to explain. It's like you inhale. You exhale. You write.

So you never struggle with your writing?

Well, there's a book of mine called *Unseen Academicals*, and that was a *Discworld* football novel. I came up with the idea years and years ago, and it didn't work. So I forgot about it. Then, quite a long time afterwards, I suddenly realised that a football novel isn't necessarily about football, but it's about the people who play football and the effect it has on their lives. So it had been gestating over a period and suddenly there it was popping up. So I just realised how it worked. I suppose most of what I do, that's how it works really.

So how long does it take you to write a book? Has it become quicker and easier over the years?

It takes longer these days because people keep ringing me up. [*Laughs*] Because it's now a business. Agents want you to do things and publishers want you to do things and people want to come and visit and all that sort of stuff. In the very beginning, when it was just me, I had left 'paid for' work as it were, I was bringing books out really fast because no one had found out where I lived!

How important would you say the title is for your books? Do you come up with titles before you write or do you have a working title?

Well, with *The Unseen University*, for example, there was a whole lot of fun in that. Half of the teachers in my school got into that, including Mr Bissett, the games master: "The boy who doesn't bring his football kit, must play in his pants!" That's what he would say. I was very good at the 'note from your mum'. Actually I would say that writing is a process of breaking yourself and everything you've done into little bits and pasting them on something else. That's how it seems to work.

With book titles, do you change them very often? Or do they pretty much stick?

The Colour of Magic was the first one that was immediately a bestseller. *The Light Fantastic* followed quite quickly. *I Shall Wear Midnight* – that was a children's book that adults read as well – the title for that just dropped into my mind.

So what do you do in a typical writing day?

Carry on with the work-in-progress, usually. I have PCA [*Posterior Cortical Atrophy*]. It's a type of Alzheimer's. It's a kind of Rolls-Royce of Alzheimer's, as someone said. What I do is dictate to my computer. The technology on it is pretty good for a first draft.

I have a PA, and at the moment when you rang, what we were doing was working on a first draft, because I think that it's on the second or third draft that the magic really happens. I very much like talking to the computer because it seems a natural thing to do.

Do you imagine when you're talking to the computer that it's a person you're telling the story to, or do you inhabit your characters?

I suppose I'm just talking to the ether itself – whatever's out there. Or to Narrativia, my patron goddess, who has got a little shine to her!

You mentioned before about characters you know appearing in your books. Do you ever worry about libel or do you just take little aspects of characters and then draw on those?

It's all about the commonality of mankind. I mean, no particular person is one alone. I remember looking out of a cab in London and seeing myself on a bicycle. I knew it looked just like me and I thought, 'I didn't know I was here today.' People who appear in my books are generally ones that wanted to be in there. On occasions, they've actually paid money. There was a vogue for this – not just with me but also with other writers, even posh writers – some time ago to pay to be a character in the next book for a payment to charity.

So, of course, the mechanism of all that is that you say: once they're in the writer's hands they might be a killer. And they say, "Oh, good! I'd like to be a killer!"

So who has paid to be in your books? Are you able to share more?

The names would not mean anything to you. You have read a *Discworld* book, I assume? Did someone sit you down and force you?

No. [*Laughs*] My father recommended it years ago.

In Ankh-Morpork, they have a 'Seamstresses' Guild', and if you know how this sort of thing works, it actually means it's a brothel. Still following me? Although, actually it's run by the girls themselves. There was one husband who paid quite a lot for his wife to be one of them. She wanted to be in it as well. Fantasy and science fiction have fandoms! Though they're not so fan-ish as you might think – they're quite pleasant people, really.

You've sold over 85 million copies of your books. If you had to define the ingredients – we've covered some of them already – what would you say it is about your books that really draws people in?

I get asked this all the time; it's always a difficult one. What happens so many times is that someone will come up to me and say that either they or their child had never read a book for fun until they picked up *Colour of Magic* or one of my books, and now the whole family's reading them. I get that often. I've lost track of the times when it's the mother saying that, usually their boy never touched a book until he read mine. In one particular case, he is now a professor in a university, which I rather like. I don't know: I just put into it all the stuff that I'd like to put into it.

So, you just have tremendous fun while you're writing?

Yes! Yes, absolutely! It's obscene isn't it really?

Not at all! That's exactly how it should be. You've mentioned that your writing is more of a business now. Do you enjoy that?

Well, you don't say, "I'm going to put this in because it's going to be worth a few dollars" or something like that. The book itself is the thing.

Do you enjoy marketing and promoting your books as much as writing them?

Not so much now. In the early days, when they sent you out with some tickets and a list of places you'd got to go to and sign books or talk to people, I did. It was better in the early days because you're more or less a free agent. But now sometimes, you know, you sometimes feel as if you're property: property of the publishers and property of the readers, really.

Have you ever thought about trying a completely different genre under a completely different name?

It would still be me. I would find my way out. You would still see me crashing out of it! So I balance it between writing for kids and writing for adults. And the nice thing is, it's crossover.

If you started again, is there anything that you would do differently?

Not really. It's one of these questions that hasn't really got a proper answer, I think. I could have probably left work, which was for the Central Electricity Generating Board [as press officer] at that particular time, much earlier. But I was married with a child then and I thought, 'I want to be careful about this. I'm not going to leave paid employment until I'm certain I've got some security for x number of years.' In fact, I had a fixed book deal from Gollancz and with that behind me, that was it. The rocket went up.

Do you have any tips for aspiring writers?

Yes, don't do what I do. Do what *they* do! One thing is read books. All books. Every book. Look at everything. It's very hard to explain how you do it. What you have to be is *you*. So don't try to be somebody else – just write with passion about subjects that you're passionate about.

One thing I found was that working on a local newspaper for several years (or actually rather more when we add all the times when I was a sub-editor), there were disciplines there that were very useful for a writer, which I didn't actually realise at the time. One of the things is: you sit in the chair and keep on doing it. You always get people saying, "I've always wanted to write a book, but I've never finished it." So you say, "Well, that's why you're not a writer. You have to get to the end of it. You send it off. You hope someone buys it." I don't think it's complicated. Though it might be difficult.

So it's about persistence and wanting it enough?

Yes, but I was never hungry for it. I mean I've read all the best writers. I actually read every bound volume of *Punch* that ever was up to the 1960s – just for the fun of it, because some of the best writing in the world was written in *Punch*. You're doing it for fun, but what you're getting is an education.

JOHN GRAY

"No publishers had wanted either book. I approached at least ten."

John Gray's groundbreaking book, *Men Are from Mars, Women Are from Venus*, is the all-time bestselling hardback non-fiction book. It changed the way men and women view relationships, and launched his *Mars-Venus* series.

John has written 23 books on relationships and personal growth and has sold over 50 million copies in 50 different languages. He's been a relationship therapist and author for over 30 years.

He lives in Northern California with his wife of 26 years. They have three daughters and three grandchildren.

Shakespeare said, "Some people are born great; some people achieve greatness; others have it thrust upon them," and this was thrust upon me.

I never thought I'd be a writer: I wanted to be a teacher. As a monk, I taught spirituality and meditation and yoga. Then, when I moved on from that, I began teaching about relationships. I'm a good counsellor, I'm a good teacher, and people said, "You should write a book. Your ideas are so unique and different." So it was that: the pressure from other people to write a book. Then I started feeling, "Okay, I have to write this book." Then, I really wanted to write this book. Then I had to learn how to write it.

When you talk about learning to write, what did that mean for you? Was it a 'process' you learned?

Well, I just sat down and I wrote a short book. In the first stages, I wasn't a good writer. What happened for me is I'm very analytical, so I would get stuck on one point and go deeper and deeper and deeper on that point and it was hard to shift to another point.

So while I was writing, I thought, 'Okay, I need to do something different.' So I thought, 'Okay, left brain is logic and reasoning. Emotion and intuition is right brain. Also, drawing pictures is right brain.' So I would draw a cute little cartoon to illustrate the point that I was making. I'd write for a while on a particular point and then I'd draw a cartoon. It was literally like training my brain to work on the right side of the brain and the left at the same time. I would draw a cartoon – which would be a little sketch with an idea behind it and a little humour with it – and then I would move on to the next page and continue writing and then draw another cartoon. I eventually refined those cartoons and published that book. That's my first book,

What You Feel, You Can Heal, which has sold over a million copies. It's not a big famous book, because it's been over 25 years since it was first published.

So I did that book and had very moderate success. People loved it, but I didn't really get a big publisher. I self-published and did get a distributor. Then it started doing much, much better, which opened the door for the distributor to distribute my next book, which was the *Mars-Venus* ideas and it was called *Men, Women and Relationships*.

So then back to the question: how did I write that one? Well, I didn't do cartoons. I finished the other book by kind of getting my left and right brain working together. But this was a book where I just put in everything I knew about relationships. It was kind of like, "Okay, I want to write just one book and be done with this because I don't like writing at all!" So I just put everything in that book. It was a big thick book and it did very well. We sold 50,000 copies through a small distributing house, and that was really good.

I did that as a partnership with a publisher, Beyond Words Publishing: I was already with the distributor that distributed the book. I wrote that big thick book and it took three years to do. It was a big, big process, and lots of late nights and everything, but I just wanted to get it done with. 'I never have to do it again,' that's what I thought! The book did so good that an agent contacted me – because I didn't have an agent and nobody had wanted to be my agent, either.

How many agents and publishers did you approach? People often ask how many rejection letters authors have received.

Yeah, they tend to. No publishers had wanted either book. I approached at least ten for both my books and nobody wanted to publish them. Beyond Words published *Men, Women and Relationships* because he was a good friend of mine and it was a small publishing house at that time. They later went on to become very, very successful with other books as well, including *The Secret*. But there are great people there.

So Men, Women and Relationships was doing 50,000 copies and an agent called me up and said, "Hey, my friend tells me you're really good and I should look at this, and that you've done really well. I think I can sell this book to New York because you've sold 50,000 on your own." Even though I did have a small publishing house with me, I should put that in. But she was considering it, "Without the big guns behind you, you did really well, so I think I can sell it based on that."

So Patti Breitman, the agent who called me up, said, "I want to bring your book to New York. I think we can sell it." I said, "Great." So I went to the Publishers Group West, which was my distributor, and I said, "Good news. New York wants to take my book." And they said, "Not good news for us, because every time we do well with a book, New York takes it over and now we don't get to distribute it." So I said, "Oh, not good news for you, the people who helped me out when I was a nobody."

So I sat there in the meeting and I listened to them tell me how they could do as good as any New York publisher. I didn't believe it, but I felt the responsibility and a loyalty to them for helping me when nobody wanted my books. So I decided it would be cruel of me to do that, insensitive. So I said, "Okay, you guys can keep this book." My wife and my agent were there and they were going, "What? Are you crazy? This is your dream, to get this to a real publisher and get it out there."

We're in the elevator going down, and I still remember the moment when my agent said, "What are you going to do?" In that moment, the thought emerged, "I'll write another book. It'll be even better." It's like a woman that has a pregnancy; the last thing she wants is another baby. I was thinking, 'I never have to write a book again.' But now it would have been really unfair of me at an emotional level; these people who helped me, I wanted to help them.

So I said, "You know, I've been doing a lot of research on this book and many people haven't even finished it. Everybody loved *Men, Women and Relationships*, but they haven't finished it. So I'm going to write a shorter version of it; I can just rewrite it. Since I wrote that book, I've done lots of media and I've found out what people like and which are the best points. So I'll just condense it down. Instead of a book that has 150 really significant points about how men and women are different and how we can get along, I'll take the top ten and I'll just make a really simple book that everybody will finish. I'll just write a shorter one this time." My agent said, "You'll write another book?" I said, "Yes." She said, "How long will it take you?" I said, "Three months." Three months is what I took for that book. She said, "Okay, based on the success of your previous book, I'll go and sell the new idea." I said, "But when you sell the new idea, it has to be the title: *Men Are from Mars, Women Are from Venus*. I won't accept anything less."

I wanted the first title to be *Men Are from Mars, Women Are from Venus*, but nobody would publish it with that title because they thought it sounded like astrology. They thought it was silly; it wasn't the right title. So as a result, I had changed it to *Men, Women and Relationships* and everybody had agreed that was a better title. This time I said, "Okay, if you sell this book in New York, I want to be able to retitle it."

So it was auctioned out. Many publishers were interested. They liked the material and they liked my success, but they didn't like the title. Finally, it was just two publishers that liked the title and liked the material. HarperCollins got the bid. That was very, very exciting for us. The next day, I started writing the book. Every week, I wrote a chapter and I was done in 12 weeks.

Excellent.

I wrote that book and that was the smoothest, easiest one to write because it was kind of just rewriting the other book but in a much easier, friendly way for people. That was the beginning of a much easier writing career for me, which was, "We can do it in three months. Next time, I'm going to do it in two months." The next time, I did it in one month, and then I wrote a book in a week. So I got really good and fast at this, because I'm not a writer who wants to sit down every day and write. I'm a talker. I like to talk to groups and talk to my clients and talk on TV shows. That's what I enjoy most.

Do you talk your books or do you write your books when you're putting them together?

I write them: every word in all my books. I don't record them. It's not like just talking freely to people when I write. I write a line and I read over that line again and again. Then another note comes, and then another line comes. I read over those two lines and I read another a few times and another note comes. Then suddenly, it just all spews out for a while and then it stops, and I have to reread the whole thing several times. Then the melody continues. Some people – the critics of my books – say it's repetitive. But the people who really want help in their relationships, they never say it's repetitive; they say it's fantastic. That's because to apply the stuff, you need to go over it again and again.

If you read it now – 25 years since I wrote it, 21 since I published it – the ideas back in those days were so controversial and were so easy to misinterpret. You had to gently repeat the idea we just covered and take another step with it, and repeat that idea and take another step with it. Today, maybe you don't need to be as repetitive, but for people who need help in their relationships, they need that repetition. That was my journey. Then after that, writing books became a much easier process for me. But that's how I learned to do it. It was trial and error.

Here's a thought that other people might be interested in: when the new agent came, I said, "Look, why don't we just get a ghostwriter to rewrite my other book?" She said to me, "John, we can get a ghostwriter. You can talk to them, but it'll be in *their* words. You have a rapport with your audience. That's why you're popular. If you don't use *your* own words in your book, they won't get you 100 percent." That really stuck with me. I said, "Okay." So I really want my message to be as authentic as it can be, so nobody changed any of the words in that book. The editor just suggested things: "Can you make this stronger? Why is this so? Would you explain this more?" that kind of thing. But I wrote every single word in that book. So it really does come through as authentically me. I think that's part of the power of that book. Because it wasn't like I just sat down and wrote. Those were the ideas that I'd been teaching for ten years up to that point, very effectively and getting great responses. If your book is based upon years and years of successfully teaching your ideas and seeing them work again and again, then it's going to be much more powerful.

How did you come across the concept of *Men Are from Mars*? Was that something you'd already been incorporating in your teaching?

The actual words of the title *Men Are from Mars* were very significant, as that was part of my teaching at a certain point. Lots of people came to me for counselling and I'd always say, "What did your other counsellor do?" I'd see what they were doing wrong. Obviously, if it didn't work, it didn't work. I thought of my own personal life and that trying to think that men and women were the same was a problem. When I would counsel men and women, what I would see is that women would misinterpret men all the time – just misinterpret them consistently. Women would often say things like, "I don't understand them," and the answers to me seemed so obvious because I'm a guy.

So I began to realise that there were these differences between men and women. There's a lot more detail to that, but as a counsellor I discovered that helping us interpret each other had a lot to do with gender. Then I began teaching that and developing all those ideas that men are from Mars. In that process, there was tremendous opposition, which kept strengthening my resolve to put it out there.

That's interesting that there was a lot of opposition.

I got knocked down by criticism. Then I went back in my counselling room and people were just so happy with the insights they were learning, and I kept seeing it working in counselling. I would go out and people would be critical of it. When I gave talks, there was always somebody that would really hate me because I was saying this, and get mad at me, saying, "You're wrong and you're patriarchal and you're sexist. I'm leaving!" I'd think, 'Wait a second. I'm trying to help a relationship by understanding differences when they show up. I'm not saying everybody has to be this way.' So the point in there is I had to sort of constantly refine my ideas so they didn't upset people.

Because it was such a controversial thing. While I was refining those ideas to not upset people, I thought, 'What if I can make this funny?' Because I was not academic in the way I presented it, but very sincere and logical. But it wasn't like people would laugh in my talks. It's not like you'd sit in the back of my room and you'd see every two to three minutes the whole audience chuckling and elbowing each other, laughing at my jokes. So I wasn't funny back then. I won't say I'm funny even now: I'd say I'm entertaining and humorous. But laughter is something you hear a lot in my talks these days. People say when they read that book, they laugh at themselves as well.

So back in the days before the ideas were accepted, and I was still learning these ideas, I kept thinking, 'How can I make this light and fun?' Because people were getting too serious about it. Then I saw the movie E.T. So later, I was in an audience of women and I said, "Women, just imagine your husband is E.T.," and they laughed. My point was, "If you're from another planet, then you wouldn't presume to correctly interpret everything. Maybe it's different customs. If you understand those customs, you can make sense of them." So that was my idea: imagine your husband's an extra-terrestrial. Even before I said it, all the women laughed, and that was a surprise to me. Then one woman said, "Where's my husband from?" And I said, "Mars." Everybody laughed again. So this is the first joke I made, and I thought, "Wow, this is great. This is lightening up the subject."

So from there, I just continued focusing on the metaphor of being from different planets and coming together. Then everything was wonderful. We learned how we're different. I talked to them about our differences. We went to Earth on a honeymoon. When we got there, everything was fine until amnesia set in and we forgot one thing: that we're from different planets. We started to expect each other to be the same. Every time I told that story, for a good eight years – at least for me, and many people in the audience – the hairs on your arm would stand up. So I always take notice whenever I get goosebumps. I think that's what happened there. It's like watching *American Idol*. At the beginning, you hear somebody singing and it's as though their talent is coming out to the world. If you get little goosebumps, you kind of know they're going to be one of the winners.

So it was definitely an idea that was a winner, and I kept repeating it, repeating it, and I thought 'once I put it in the book, then I won't have to tell that story any more'. Little did I know I'd be talking about *Men Are from Mars, Women Are from Venus* for the rest of my life. But I don't have to tell that story any more, because you can't say the same thing over and over. But I can certainly talk on the subject over and over, because I'm constantly finding better ways to say it and understanding it in new ways and applying it in different ways.

So you have a powerful voice – you're using your own voice, not a ghostwriter's voice – you've got a powerful metaphor, and you've got a catchy title. Are there any other ingredients that you think made that book such a success?

Ten years of successfully changing the lives of thousands of people with that information. That, I think, is the real essence of it. Another thing is, I'm very media-friendly. I enjoy doing media. I am always told afterwards, "Gee, you made that so easy for us." I learned how to do media really well. It comes very easily to me. That is sort of my natural talent, as opposed to being a writer.

It was a message with real substance, a proven substance for ten years. It was a catchy title. I always like to say it's not just the title. I was published in Germany with the title *Men and Women Are Different* and it sold five million copies. They thought *Men Are from Mars* was a weird title, so they didn't use it.

And it still sold five million copies. Brilliant! You say you managed to get the process of your writing down from a longer period to three months and then down eventually to a week. Can you give any tips for other writers on how you would do that?

Well, I was under a big deadline. I'd done several *Oprah* shows on a subject for which I didn't even have a book. The publishers said, "This is insanity. You have to get this book out or people are going to forget you did these shows." So there was a lot of pressure on me to get it out. Because of the pressure, deadlines are really helpful for me to shorten the time. I have to have a deadline – and they offered me a lot of money.

So, another big incentive.

Yes, big advances and deadlines are very motivating. Though I wouldn't recommend writing a book in a week. It's just that one book I wrote in a week. To write a book, my goal generally is to give three months from beginning to end, and that's a reasonable amount of time for me. But it's really a little deceptive because the ideas in the book, I'll be teaching for at least a year beforehand.

So, you have lots of planning and preparation?

Yeah. Before I sit down and actually write, I start developing the ideas. I get the idea for the book. Then I'm going to teach those ideas. I'm going to go out and do talks on those ideas. I'll be doing interviews to promote whatever book is out there. But during those interviews, I'll be trying out my new material. All the material in my books is always tested. It's tested not just in my workshops but in my counselling room and also on the media. People should know, as an author, what we have to do is take complex ideas and simplify them for people to understand. That's a skill in communication.

People who are in the media can take your simplified ideas and simplify them even more, because that's why they're the number-one talk show person. They've got drive-time shows; these people don't have much time. So you learn to make your ideas even more concise, and you can also see what they get excited about – because if they're not excited about your ideas, the other ones aren't going to promote them. So I test it with the media before I sit down. I have to say, some of the best lines I've used in my books I heard first from a media person summarising what I just said. Sometimes, they summarise what I said and it was a different point that I hadn't even thought of.

Excellent. So how much time do you spend writing your books and how much time do you spend publicising them?

Well now, it's a little different in my life. But for the first 23 books, I wrote a book every year, occasionally two books. Somewhere there's a long list of all of them. I was surprised: I did a summary of all my books and it turned out there are 23. So that was interesting.

What I did is I would teach for a year the ideas that were going to be in that book, and then I would sit down and write it in three months. That was the average to write a book on that subject. Then I'd teach the next idea. While I'm promoting that book, I'm getting an idea for the next book. Let's say I've written a book on dating: while I'm promoting the book on dating, I'm doing media. And I'm thinking from the media things, what comes up is, "You should write a book on marriage." Okay. So now I'm going to write a book on the challenges of marriage. So let me start talking about those ideas while I'm promoting the dating book.

So I constantly try to bring in the new ideas from the media in my workshops. I create a few actual workshops on that topic and work with the group. So you see, my ideas are all tested – always. Getting feedback is so important for me as writer in terms of the self-help genre. I really want to make sure it's helping people and I'm finding out what exactly is helping people the most. When I teach to my workshops, I always spend at least an hour or two at the end when I'll say, "What did you learn? What did you hear?" I learn so much from that. It's your audience who can bring up the best ideas. I'm throwing out 50 ideas: I don't know which seed is going to take. It's that response you get. It helps you with that.

It's the response from the audience and from the people that you help – your clients?

Yes. It helps to find the ideas that I would put into a book. But then, when I'm writing the book, I'm thinking about what those people said. Many of my books give examples of how those people used my ideas to help them.

That helps you decide what to take out and what to leave in, in terms of content?

Yes.

So, if you started your writing career over again, is there anything you'd change? Was there any time that was a defining moment for you?

If I knew then what I know now, what would I do? How would I help myself better? You've stumped me on that one. It seems like every step of the way was a learning experience for me to get to the place where I am now.

Well, the big defining moment is when I decided to let my publisher keep *Men, Women and Relationships*, and decided to write another book. That was a huge turning point for me. I was really grateful to my agent, who would constantly lean on me to write another book. I'm the kind of person that needs a little bit of outside stimulation to do something. I'd be happy to sit on my laurels unless somebody says, "Hey, we need you."

Would you advise other writers, if they're really passionate about a subject, to ignore the rejections of publishers – to just keep going and believe in themselves?

Well, I certainly had to do that. Though I don't fully ignore them: I get a little beat up by it and then I pick myself back up. There's information that's important to take in. But the overall thing is: if somebody doesn't like you, don't listen to the feedback. If somebody likes you, listen to the feedback. But even when people didn't like me and gave negative feedback, I would read it. I read everything I could that people said about me and tried to understand their point of view. The whole thing is, if somebody is opposing you, *why* are they opposing you? At least try to understand their perspective. That's hard when somebody's criticising you at that point. It's much easier when somebody likes you and is nice about it.

There were always negative things said about me in different interviews all the way during the first five years of my book being on the bestseller list. There weren't really any 'love letter' interviews where people just said nice things about me. Now I get lots of those. But in those days, I didn't get any. It was like rejection again and again.

You can go on amazon.com; I'm probably one of the biggest sellers that's ever sold on amazon.com. Look at a review they have up there. It's a crummy, stupid review of my book saying it's no good. I'm thinking, 'Come on. Look at all the good reviews since. Why don't you put a new one on?' They said, "Nope, that's a legitimate review. We're keeping it there."

How do you cope with that, with negative criticism?

Well, I wrote a book on that. [*Laughs*] The information is in a book called *Mars and Venus Starting Over*. It's a similar situation. Taking criticism is like having someone die or having a marriage end: it's your heart that's broken. You put your heart and soul into something and somebody rejects you, it breaks your heart. So how do you heal a broken heart? In a small way, I did it over and over and over. It's in a much bigger way when somebody dies or if your marriage falls apart. But it's the same tools I used to pick myself up again and again, which is to come back to your dream. Come back to your innocence.

William Blake talked about life having three stages: innocence, experience, and if you're lucky, having had experience to return to innocence. That's what I've had to do again and again: you sort of get beat down by criticism and rejection and negativity, and your heart closes and you have to open it back up and believe in yourself again. The process in doing that has various aspects to it. But one aspect is to explore the feelings that come up and understand them and find forgiveness.

I remember something that was very helpful for me once. I was doing a tour of Europe and I spent two days just doing one interview after another. I thought, 'Why can't we do one press conference and I'll deal with everybody?' But no, everybody had to have a private interview with me, asking me questions. They all seemed so sincere and positive. Then the articles came out and all of them had several jabs, big jabs, against me and sounded cynical. I thought, 'Wow, what a betrayal.' Because I thought these people liked me and I was being friendly and nice with them. Then they'd say mean things about me like, "He just wants to do it for the money. He's laughing on his way to the bank." Just critical things.

So I was teaching on a seminar that weekend and I invited the press to come for free. One of the press people was there and I was sharing that experience with her. She said, "John, if you look at the articles, we do say some positive things, but we can't sell our articles to get printed if we don't say negative things." So I said, "Okay. Well, that's life." She said, "Don't take it so personally," and gradually I learned not to take it personally. But I had to do my own internal work. Whenever somebody is criticising you, you fear that you might be wrong. You feel the fear and let it go, and you feel the sadness that you don't have all the answers, and you feel the anger that they betrayed you in some way or that they're not liking you in some way. What I've found is that always, whenever there's a knockdown and you feel a blow to your ego, you have these natural emotional reactions. If you process them, as I talk about in my books, then you can let go of them quite easily. So I'm almost invincible. I've taken it all and I just keep moving forward now. I keep focusing on the good and listen to the bad, but I don't let it stop me.

You mentioned the importance of the media in promoting your books. Do you have any tips for authors who are trying to get media publicity for their books?

Here's a good encouraging thought I'd say to aspiring authors: don't be afraid of the radio or TV media. TV and radio is 'visual': it's all about looking good. With written media, there's no visuality. So a writer can anonymously criticise you and sound negative and it's just words. But with the radio and TV, it's different. A TV interviewer, first of all, is less likely to feel jealous of you because they don't feel they'll ever write a book. So they have tremendous admiration for you already. When you go on radio and TV, you go from being an expert at something to an authority. That's where you want to get to, where you're an authority. If you get on a TV or radio show, just because you have written a book and they haven't, they go, "Wow." They want to look good by making you look good. That's what people should remember: it's in their interest to make you look good. When I remind people of that, it takes away a lot of their fear.

When you're doing radio and TV, you should just have three points. That's it. You should learn those three points, and practise them. No matter what question they ask, you always give your three points. They're thinking about the next question they're going to ask. They're not going to say, "You didn't answer my question. What's the answer?" You could say, "That's a really a good question," and make your points. Or somebody might ask, "What do you say to all the critics of your book?" Answer, "That's a very good question, because there has been some criticism. Most people believe that this book is incredible and all that I hear is how wonderful the book is. The reason people think it's so wonderful is because men and women are different. And quite often, we don't understand those differences. Then we have misinterpretations – lack of understanding, and unnecessary friction results. So we have to take time to understand these differences and then communication works better." That could have been one of my main points.

So what I did was avoid that question completely and gave the point I wanted to make about my book, being very much aware of my audience. I'm thinking: why would my audience want to buy my book? So I'm giving three points for why they would want to buy my book. Each point has to be something that a person hasn't thought of before, something interesting, to create a need for my book.

If I wrote *The Nine Secrets of Happiness*, I would never list all nine in a media interview. What if they asked me, "What are the nine secrets of happiness?" I would answer, "Well, I can certainly let you know the first three, and I will talk about those three." Because people cannot remember more than three points – anything more than that, they're going to forget your first point. Keep it simple. No matter what questions they ask, come back to your point. "That's a good point. What I hear is ... and what I think is ... and one of the best ideas that I put in this book is ..." It doesn't have to relate to the question. You just make sure you give your three points every time. That's a thing to remember.

Before I write a book, I'll start trying it out with the media. I'll get on media promoting one book, but now I'm doing a new subject. I'll start talking about some of the new ideas in my new book and then I'm hearing the feedback of the radio person. So I'm already getting the experience of whether they're interested in it and what they're interested in – because they're the people that you want to promote your book, the people on radio and TV.

Of course, now we have blogs and so forth. But it's important to test your ideas out via whatever avenue you have. Back in those days, it was just radio and TV to promote books. Now it's a whole other world. You may want to do Facebook and your website and your blogs and all that, but you're still getting feedback.

What's so challenging for people today is that the negative feedback on the web can just be so torturing. But you also get good stuff too. What I used to do was to go into different chat rooms and give my material anonymously, even for the later books. I'd never say: it's John Gray, author of *Men Are from Mars*. I would just go in there and try out my new material anonymously.

People would say, "Who are you? That was a really good idea. I like that," and that would give me encouragement with new ideas.

Fantastic. Do you have any other tips for aspiring authors or published authors?

Here's another thing I say to people: whatever your goals are in life, the world believes in you to the extent that you believe in yourself. To grow your muscles and believe in yourself means you have to be challenged. If I want my muscles to grow, I go to the gym and I challenge them. I don't take on a light weight; I take on a heavy weight. I don't take it all the time. I take it a bit and I rest, and I take it a bit more and I rest. Then your muscles grow stronger.

It's the same thing when you hit criticism and rejection. That forces you to believe in yourself more, and that's how you grow in your self-belief. One is you pick yourself back up, but you don't face that rejection all the time. You take a break from it and you take time to be with the people who do believe in you. So you have to have a supportive group of people who believe in you. The more people you can associate with who have achieved some of their goals and dreams the better, as opposed to a bunch of people who haven't.

ALEXANDER McCALL SMITH

"The title of the book is absolutely crucial to its success, so you've got to get the right title."

Photo by Chris Watt

Alexander McCall Smith, CBE, wrote over 30 children's books before *The No. 1 Ladies' Detective Agency* became a massive bestseller.

His various series of books have been translated into over 40 languages and sold over 40 million copies around the world.

He's received numerous awards for his writing, including the British Book Awards' Author of the Year in 2004.

When I was eight, I sent off a manuscript to a publisher, which was a bit precocious. [*Laughs*] Children write little stories, and this one I thought was a bit of a book, and was presumably only a few pages. It was the first one I sent off to a publisher, which was a bit of a cheek! I liked books, and I had the desire that so many children have, to write. I continued to do that: I remember making little books, again, as children do. I suppose that probably is the origin of my career as a writer, or my desire to write, which has continued with me for the rest of my life.

Your mother wrote, didn't she?

My mother was never published, but she did spend her time writing a massive novel, page after page, but she never let anybody see it. Again, lots of people do that. They have a drawer somewhere where they've written something, and I think for many people it's almost the equivalent of keeping a diary. Writing can be quite therapeutic; you express your views about the world and so on.

You wrote 30 books before you wrote *The No. 1 Ladies' Detective Agency*. Tell me a little about those.

I wrote over 30 children's books. I started off and wrote quite a lot of short stories, I wrote for the radio and so on. My first book published was a children's book, so I continued to do that for some years, whilst at the same time writing short stories, some of which were published or broadcast.

When you wrote *The No. 1 Ladies' Detective Agency*, the first print run was for something like 1,500 copies …

That's right, the very first run was 1,500 copies. It was published initially in 1998, in Scotland, by Polygon. It was then quite a small imprint owned by Edinburgh University Press and they did general titles. Prior to that, apart from the children's books, I had had a collection of short stories published by Canongate in Edinburgh, and another one which was a collection of African stories retold, which was also published by Canongate, and then *The No. 1 Ladies' Detective Agency* was published by Polygon.

If you had to pin anything down, to creating the phenomenal success of that book, what would you attribute it to?

That is probably a slightly awkward question for the author to answer! I think that the character of Mma Ramotswe appealed. Here was a person without guile, who was very sympathetic and kind, and I think people like that sort of character in fiction. They're often happy to discover a character who they actually like in a book. I think that probably was a major factor. It also was a gentle book; there wasn't anything which people found shocking or disturbing. Mma Ramotswe was concerned with fairly ordinary matters, day-to-day matters, and she represented an approach to life, which was conciliatory and comfortable for people.

You've said before that the larger your readership, the more you lose ownership over your characters. Can you expand on this?

Yes, I think that's right. If you send out a set of literary characters into the world, you suddenly realise that they've become the property or the friends of the people who read about them. Fictional characters – of course we know that they don't exist – but people have a relationship with them.

It's almost a sort of assumption that these people are in a way real for the reader. So the characters have what amounts to an independent existence, an existence which is independent of the creator of the character. Once Mma Ramotswe and the other characters in the books became quite popular, I realised that I was just a custodian of those lives. It's quite an interesting matter, but yes, that happened.

What kind of writing routine do you have? You're quite prolific: you write four or five books a year and something like 1,000 words per hour.

I have to write just about every day. You have to keep to a plan because, in my case with four or five books a year, I have four or five deadlines. So there's about two or three months allocated to each book. What happens then is that means I have to keep at it, so I will write for about three hours a day, sometimes a bit longer. On a good day it might be 4,000 words, but more often it's going to be about 3,000 words a day.

Of course, I have a lot of other commitments. I've got a lot of projects and we get lots of correspondence and other matters that have to be dealt with, so my days are fairly full. I tend to start quite early; I prefer to write in the morning. I can write at other times of the day, but morning seems to be the best time. Often it's very early, so I will get up in the summer at four o'clock and write until half past six or seven. So by the time most people are getting out of bed, I've possibly done my allocated writing for the day.

Do you set yourself a target for the day?

I usually think I must do between 2,000 or 3,000 words a day, depending on where we are in the book. Then I will do that: I have to do that.

How important is the title to you?

I think the title of the book is absolutely crucial to its success, so you've got to get the right title. That, of course, is something that requires quite a bit of thought. Sometimes you get a title which you know instinctively, right at the very beginning, is the right title for a book and you say, "Well, I can't call it anything but this." When that happens, that view tends to be shared by the publishers, and that's usually because the title has some very obvious merits to it. I discuss titles with my editors, but particularly with my editor in New York. We have a very good title conversation about every book, more or less, which is good fun. He suggests a different adjective and I get back to the drawing board, and so on. So that's the way that works.

You mentioned having a plan for your book. Is that comprehensive or is it just a series of bullet points?

In the case of some books, I'll have a general structure, but I may not have anything particularly written down. I'll know roughly what the major plotlines will be. So when I start a new Mma Ramotswe book – I'm writing a Mma Ramwotse book at the moment, for example – I will know what the main plotlines will be, but I won't have planned in detail how those reveal themselves or anything of that sort.

Do you have any rituals or anything that helps you write day-to-day?

Not really, no. I do have music that I play, and that is quite important for me. I think that music does seem to help. I know there are different views on that, but there is some evidence that listening to music actually unlocks creative and constructive parts of the brain.

What exactly do you listen to?

Well, it's certainly eclectic. It's obviously not going to be anything terribly harsh or distracting, so it tends to be on the classical side. I've got eclectic taste, though it's not pop music. I may listen to choral music, I may listen to operatic arias. I've just been writing and I was listening to very nice Icelandic singers. There are all sorts of things.

At last count, you'd written 96 books, but I imagine it's probably more than that by now.

I've actually genuinely stopped counting. I know that that sounds affected, but I really have. So I don't know how many I've written.

There have been some huge changes in publishing over the last ten years. What do you think about those?

I suppose there are some changes which I would be concerned about, and which I would think would be changes to be regretted. I think that if publishing becomes large and impersonal, and the relationship between the author and the publisher is made less of a personal one, that would be a very bad thing. I think that that, to an extent, might be happening. The idea of having a publisher who believes in a book and who supports the author and is very aware of what the author wants to do, all of that is very positive. The close relationship between publisher and author is a great working relationship. If that is compromised by publishing becoming more impersonal, with larger publishing firms dominating the scene, that I think would be a great pity. It would give little room for the quirky; little room for inspired choices on the part of an editor, and so on.

Do you have any thoughts about the rise of e-publishing and Kindle books?

I think that if people want to read books on their Kindles, and they find that that is the easiest and most attractive way to do it, then that's fine. There is every indication that people are buying books in e-form, and that it hasn't led to the demise of publishing. I think, in a way, the conventional printed book is better for most purposes because it's always there for you to see and handle as an aesthetic experience. Handling a beautifully produced book, it's an object of beauty. It's also probably a little bit easier to share it. People probably don't share e-books in the same way that they share an actual physical book. I prefer the physical book and I prefer it quite markedly, but I understand the attraction to e-books, and e-books should be part of the overall picture.

Some of the authors I'm speaking to are saying as much as 60 percent of their books are now sold as e-books.

As high as that? That's interesting. I don't think it's that in my case, but I think that will depend on a particular author's demographic and a particular author's readership and so on. It also depends upon the sort of book. There are probably some sorts of books that are read more in e-formats than others. There are all sorts of variables.

They did give me some figures in America, and I'm afraid I can't recall what they said, but it's a majority of real, physical books, though quite a lot are sold in e-format.

Do you keep an eye on which forms of promotion are the most effective for selling your books? Do you have a feeling for that?

Well, I'm aware of promotional issues, but I don't really have strong views on the efficacy. I would not be able to answer if you said, "Is a newspaper advertisement more effective than a review?" I would have no idea. I'm sure the marketing people will know that. I certainly do a lot on behalf of my publishers, and to a very great extent, I do various things they want to promote the books. I'm always happy to play my part in that.

What I do know about is: I do a lot of touring. I do at least two US tours a year; I do quite a number of small tours in the UK; and then I go to Australia, and all over the world, really. So I'm aware of that, and I'm aware of the significance of appearing in public. For example, if I do a large event where I've got 600 or 700 people at it, I think you would probably multiply the number of people that you're talking to through that event by a factor of three or four – because every person that you see at an event is obviously going to talk about it to friends and so on. So you're reaching perhaps thousands of people when you speak to 500 or 600. So I think that is worth doing. It's also part of the general contact with readers that is very important. I do that very carefully and I believe in it, not just out of reasons for trying to promote books, but also out of common courtesy. If readers are in touch with me, I try to be in touch with them. When I go to events, I meet as many people as are prepared to meet me. I think that's very important, and you get feedback from the readers as well. I feel with my books that it's almost a club, really, and that there are large numbers of people all over the place who are mutual friends of the characters in my books.

Publishers are increasingly saying, "Don't bother with book tours, send out a tweet!" Do you also do promotion online?

Well, I do that. I put out tweets on Twitter. I suppose I've done a fair amount of that. I do find Facebook very useful, and I enjoy that. I enjoy Facebook a bit more because I have a page there, which I put postings on, which will be my observations on various things and news about the new books, etc. I put on excerpts from books I'm writing at the time, and I find that a very nice way of being in touch with the readers. So I think that is even more effective than a conventional website. A conventional website can be quite static; Facebook is so interactive and is real social media in the sense that you're really all involved in communication with one another in that way, so that's good.

You mentioned having feedback from readers on Facebook or Twitter, do you also have a blog?

No, I haven't got a separate blog. The one on the website, the publishers do. I don't have a blog; I treat Facebook as that. What I put on the Facebook page would be the equivalent of that. There will be comments on things and it's the equivalent of a longish blog entry.

Is your writing influenced at any stage by the feedback you're getting from readers?

Yes, I think it can be. That's particularly the case if one is writing several novels, because the readers will have views on characters and what might happen to the characters. So I'm aware of that, and that is something that, probably, subliminally, I take into account, even if I don't actually respond in clear and unequivocal terms to a suggestion. Maybe they're in the background and may affect what I write. So yes, the readers' views about the content will be views that I'm aware of. They may also say, "Oh, we're looking forward to this; why doesn't such-and-such happen?" and there have been cases where I've thought, 'Yes, exactly! Why not?' So it's been readers' suggestions, which have had a very direct effect on the way in which the plot's developed.

Do you think it's important to take readers' thoughts on board and to have a dialogue with the readers?

Yes and no. I certainly look very seriously at everything the readers say. But ultimately, one is writing the book oneself – it's not a committee. I would always say that I have the ultimate responsibility for what happens in the story, obviously, and I don't want to be too swayed. If a reader turned on a particular character in a way which I disapproved of, I wouldn't respond by also turning on the character. I maintain my responsibility as an author.

You do a lot of book tours … How much time would you say percentage-wise you spend writing compared to promoting your books?

It would be very difficult for me to hazard a guess at that. Quite a lot of my time is spent promoting the books. I've just been to America. I did a two-and-a-half-week tour in America, came back, then shortly afterwards I went to South Africa and did the Franschhoek Literary Festival outside Cape Town. Now I'm back from that and I'm going back to Hay tomorrow, doing bookstore events in Chepstow and Hay, then I come back and do the Borders Book Festival the following week, and then I go to the Althorp Literary Festival. So it continues.

It must interrupt the flow of writing.

Well it can, but we try to achieve a balance. I try to have tranches of time where I am not going to be touring or doing anything of that sort.

What about other challenges or frustrations that you have day-to-day?

Well, I don't think that one should ever say life is plain sailing, because Nemesis stalks around and waits to hear comments like that, and she says, "I'll show him." I live under fairly considerable pressure. Once you're doing four to five books a year, which is what I'm doing now, that's not simple. So I live under that sort of pressure. To an extent, your life becomes public property – it's not entirely, but you do get a bit of that. I suppose you're conscious of that, and you lose anonymity. I will be approached by people in the streets or restaurants, or whatever. Usually it's very nice, and it always seems to be very nice people who say, "We're enjoying that series" or whatever, but you're conscious of the fact that you're sometimes looked at with interest by people you don't know. That's generally okay, though I've had one or two occasions where that hasn't been exactly easy. I haven't had any major problems with that; I haven't had anything too distressing.

You're writing four or five books a year. Is there ever a point at which you think, 'Damn it, I'm only going to do one book this year?'

Well, I do so enjoy writing, I so enjoy the books that I write, that I don't really feel that. On the contrary, I want to go back to each series and say, "I haven't done a book in that series in a while and I'm looking forward to doing it." If anything, it's the other way! [*Laughs*]

You wish you could write *more* books?

Yes!

If you could go back to yourself ten or 15 years ago, is there anything you would tell yourself to do differently?

Oh, yes. Everybody should say that about their existence ten or 15 years ago. If you don't actually say that, it means that you haven't learned anything. So yes, you'd have to do that. We would all identify things about life we would do differently with the benefit of hindsight or with the benefit of the rather increased understanding of the world that you should get as each year goes past.

What are your top tips for aspiring authors?

I would say persist. Persistence is of the essence. Follow the heart and persist. It can be so discouraging to people who want to write and they encounter indifference to their efforts. They encounter the sheer problem of breaking into print. I suppose modern methods of communication have made it a little bit easier for people to see their work in print – for example, publishing things on the web constitutes the democratisation of the publishing process and print process. That sort of thing is probably a little bit easier for people in that respect, but it's certainly not easier in any way for them to get publication in book form. So I would say, persist.

I also would say to people who wish to break into print that it's actually quite important not to get fixated on that first effort, because some people write something and then they spend years doing further drafts of it. I'm of the view that if you write something, you should try to move on as soon as possible to the next thing and get practice writing the next thing. That's very important, and an important thing that I think people might perhaps like to think about at the beginning of their careers as writers.

You once said you spent the early years of your success pinching yourself because you couldn't quite believe it was real. Do you still feel like that?

There were occasions, certainly at the beginning, where I thought, 'Has this really happened?' I think that is probably what anybody would feel if suddenly their life changes, and changes in a way which they've wanted it to change. So yes, certainly, I did at times think, 'Really? Has this happened?' But I don't do that now; I've got more used to it. You get used to doing the things that you do in this life.

JOANNE HARRIS

"In a world where social media is prominent, they don't just want the books – they want to know about you."

Kyte Photography

Joanne Harris is best known for writing *Chocolat*, which has been published in over 50 countries and has sold around 30 million copies worldwide.

The book was made into a movie starring Juliette Binoche, Johnny Depp and Judi Dench, and was nominated for five Oscars.

Since then, all her novels have been bestsellers.

I don't think you can become a writer, and I don't think you set out to become a writer, or at least I don't know many people who have. I wrote; I've always written. I wrote a lot of stuff that wasn't published, and then I wrote something that was. About 15 years later, I gave up the job I was doing and I became a full-time writer, but there are so many ways of getting there.

Do you see yourself as a writer first and foremost, or a storyteller first and foremost? Or perhaps something else – some authors say they're marketers or speakers, first and foremost.

I don't put labels on myself and I generally don't encourage other people to. I'm very, very unlikely to be a marketer, because there are departments in publishing to do that and I'm really not all that interested in selling stuff. I tell stories, I write books. Whether that makes me a writer or a storyteller, I really don't mind. It depends on how people perceive me.

Why do you think you became a writer in the first place? What was it that intrigued you? Is it because you enjoyed reading other people's books, or you just love telling stories?

I loved writing. I think if you enjoy reading, then you should be a reader. Obviously, I don't think you can write unless you read, but there are plenty of people who read who aren't motivated to write, in the same way there are plenty of people who enjoy watching football and don't necessarily want to play. I've always written because I loved it. Regardless of whether I've been paid or published or any of those other things, I've always liked it.

What was the earliest thing you can remember writing?

I wrote very early, when I was seven or eight. The earliest thing I really remember writing was a long Rider Haggard-like story when I was about nine or ten, and a lot of the things I wrote at the time were very derivative, basically copying other people. A lot of muscular 'boys' own' adventure stuff because that's what I liked.

Do you have a plan when you write? There's always a dividing line between writers who have a plan and plan everything out meticulously, and people who write more organically and just see where the plot takes them.

I think everybody has a plan. It's not necessarily the same kind of plan, but I don't believe that anybody actually starts off with no ideas at all and just does automatic writing. I don't plan particularly, I usually have a general trajectory of what I've got, but there are many details, which will fill themselves in as I go along. There is something about the meticulously constructed piece of writing, which tends to kill off spontaneity and surprise. I don't want to do that, so I let the story evolve but it evolves along the path that I've already more or less figured out.

Do you get to a stage where you're actually inhabiting your characters and dreaming about your characters and believing almost that you *are* your characters?

I don't see how I can expect a reader to do it if I don't. If you're not able to believe in the reality of your characters and the emotional realism of your plot, then it's not going to be that good a plot.

How do you feel when you write? Do you still feel excited and enthusiastic, or are there days where you just don't feel the urge to write?

If I don't feel the urge to write, I don't write. I don't think anybody feels 100 percent motivated all the time. I still enjoy it; otherwise I wouldn't have done it. There are a lot better ways of making money than writing books. There are a lot easier ways of not making any money, too. It's not really something that requires motivation. It's always something I've just done. Some days it's easier than others.

From where do you draw inspiration?

Everywhere. I don't think that inspiration is something you have to go looking for; I think it finds you. I'm interested in people, places and events. I find inspiration in the people I meet and places I go: in books, in newspapers and in the news. I don't think it's difficult to find. Inspiration is everywhere.

You've described writing as, "a kind of voodoo". Can you elaborate on that?

Well, it is voodoo! How else could you make marks on a piece of paper and cause somebody across the other side of the world to react – to cry, to smile, or to want to eat chocolate? I don't know of anything else that does that, that's the power of words. I think it's as close to voodoo as we're going to get.

Can you describe your typical writing day or writing week?

I don't have one because I travel so much and do so many different things. I might get a couple of dozen "typical" days a year; that doesn't make them typical any more. If I'm here, I'll work in my shed. If I'm not here – which is increasingly the case – I'll manage and do what I can. I've long since given up expecting perfect conditions or typical conditions or any kind of routine because that doesn't seem to happen.

Do you write by hand or on a typewriter?

I have a laptop; I'm not quite that decrepit yet.

[*Laughs*] Do you set yourself a writing target per day of a certain number of words?

No, I don't see the point. I could write 10,000 words and they could be rubbish, and I would've met my target but I'd have achieved nothing. I don't see the point of setting targets that might not achieve anything. My target is to do what I can, when I can. I don't obsess about word counts or pages or hours spent doing whatever, because ultimately, no one cares how you get there. It's just the fact of getting there that matters.

How many times would you say you redraft or recraft each page or chapter?

It depends on the book. As a general rule of thumb, I don't redraft until I've got a first draft, but I do reread everything that I wrote the previous session and I tend to clean it up as I go along. Then when I've got a first draft, I will redraft it from the beginning, and then I will redraft it again for my editor. I may possibly have another look at it for, let's say, my American editor if they have different ideas or if they haven't managed to get their head together with my English editor. But that'll be it. So, four drafts, maybe.

Other authors have mentioned how they started out writing books and it increasingly became a 'business'. Do you feel that has happened, or have you tried to stay in touch with the initial urge of writing?

I don't understand what they mean by writing being a business. I genuinely don't know what that means. If it felt like a business, I'm pretty sure I wouldn't want to do it. I already had a job, which was perfectly fine, and I gave that up to write. If it turned into just another job, I don't see why I would want to continue. I don't think my mind operates in that way. There is a business side of it, and I'm very happy for other people to look after it and for me to not have to know anything about it.

You wrote two other books before your incredible success with *Chocolat*. You also did a lot of other writing before you started getting published. Tell me a little bit about those years, for other people who perhaps are still writing books without success?

I don't understand what people mean by "without success". Those books were published. At the time, that was the greatest success I could aspire to. Before that, I'd written other things that hadn't been published. But I still didn't consider them not to be a success. There's a general feeling that if it's not published, you get nothing out of it or if it's not successfully published and widely promoted, then it's not worth doing. I'm amazed that anybody writes at all, if that's how they think! I enjoyed the process. I learned a lot from the process. My first book was published to, shall we say, a cult audience, which meant it was largely unread. I was absolutely delighted; I didn't aspire to anything else. I was extremely surprised when my third book did so well, because my first two had met with the sort of reception that a paperback original with no promotion budget generally tends to meet with. I thought, 'Hey, this is what I'm doing; if it stays this way, that's fine.' I wasn't planning to give up my teaching job, which I loved, to write full time. I just kind of got pushed into it by the success of *Chocolat*, which made it clear from an early stage that there was no way that I was going to be able to do a teaching job and have this phenomenon going on. So I gave up teaching, without necessarily feeling that I was leaving it for good. I actually genuinely thought at the time that I would probably go back.

How did you handle all of the media attention and publicity at the time? Did you have any training?

I would love to know who provides training for this kind of thing. No, I didn't. I don't know anybody who has. The thing with writing is everybody prepares you for rejection, because rejection is most often what you can expect. I don't think anybody prepares you for success! So I just dealt with it because it was there to deal with. I don't live in London; I don't have the kind of lifestyle that means that I get stalked by people and followed by the press and those sorts of things. Except for quite a brief moment when the movie was up for Oscars, and suddenly there was a huge amount of interest in the book – but it's still a book. So the literary world was interested, but let's face it, the literary world is not a very big world, compared to let's say, the world of TV and cinema. So it wasn't something that I felt I needed help with, as such. It took me a little while to adjust to doing it for a living and to promoting books, and to go out and talk about them. That was quite odd, because I hadn't had to do that with my first two books. Nobody had suggested promotion or touring or book signings or anything like that – it just didn't happen. So all that was a bit new.

What would you say have been your main challenges as a writer over the years?

I'm not sure I'm capable of seeing it as being a challenge. I don't do it because it's a challenge; I do it because I love it. I'm not trying to test myself or prove anything.

I suspect by challenge you mean problems. My problems have been almost entirely practical ones: things to do with agents, money people and business people. I think dealing with that aspect of writing is not something that writers find easy, because most writers are not business people. Most writers don't want to be thought of as a business or a product. I think it's fairly normal for writers to believe that their agents and their editors and people who work for them are actually their friends. It's not necessarily true, and I think you have to be just a little bit careful of making that assumption. At least, this is what I would tell my younger self.

You mentioned that you don't want to be thought of as 'a product', and indeed many authors might agree with that. Do you think there's a tension between where publishers and literary agents are coming from and authors who might have a more artistic vision?

I think a good agent knows how to take that in their stride. Publishers, it depends on the department. A lot of authors I know are not entirely comfortable with the marketing side or the sales side, because I think to them it seems a little crude. Agents are generally pretty good at walking the line. A good agent will know how to handle the business side of something and how to handle the ego side of something. Writers generally have egos, and some have bigger egos than others.

Have there been any significant turning points in the way you've tackled books or understood publishing?

Or have there been any other moments of enlightenment over the years?

I'm not sure it comes to me in moments of enlightenment. I think with every book I've felt that I needed to try something slightly different. I think that's not typical in a lot of writers. Many writers either want to, or are more or less forced to by their publishers, to do pretty much the same thing over and over again. I resisted that, and it hasn't always been easy, because the bigger you get, the more of a sense of expectation. I've tried to combat these expectations, so I've done lots of different things. As a result, there's always been a little bit of uncertainty between my publishers and me. They're very good and they've supported me in all the things that I've done, but I'm pretty sure that they would've loved for me just to write about chocolate forever.

What do you think about the changes in publishing over the last ten years – things like promotion on the Internet, social media, and virtual book tours?

I think they're just fine. I think publishers tend to do them rather poorly, and the people who do them best are authors themselves. I'm still not convinced that publishers are brilliant in terms of dealing with these things. I think they're a bit backward with social media. They still think that making a Facebook page is a really cool idea, whereas if you look at the people who work social media extremely well, they're doing all sorts of things that publishers wouldn't be able to do and wouldn't see the point of doing. Personally, I like social media. I enjoy using it and I use it to my advantage and it works for me, but I'm not sure it's the best thing for publishers to do. I'm not really sure that it helps all that much in some cases.

Obviously, the big change has been electronic media and electric books. Here again, I think publishing has been quite slow to pick up the potential of this. When I first signed up for Transworld, the idea of e-books was so nebulous, and there was a general feeling in the business that it would be a faddy thing that would never take off. Agents were selling e-book rights left, right, and centre; or worse, giving them for free! This happened to everybody. This wasn't very long ago – it was only 13 years ago. E-book rights were just being given for free as part of 'rights' packages. It was like audiobook rights – who really cared? It's become enormous now. It's become a whole new way of buying and perceiving books.

It will get bigger and bigger, I think. Again, I think publishers are always one step behind on this. They're doing their best, but there should've been some foresight at the time. There should have been some work done on the emerging area of e-books. I don't think anybody actually did it, with the result that it took publishing slightly by surprise, and publishing is now very insecure because of it. Because quite rightly, the publishers understand that all it would take would be for Amazon, for instance, to headhunt some really good editors and establish a really good editorial service for their Kindle store, and all of the sudden, you'd have potentially the biggest publisher and distributor in the world out there.

You're quite active on Twitter, aren't you? Do you use other social media to keep in touch with your readers and promote your books? How useful do you find it?

I use Tumblr and Twitter, and I've got a website. Yes, I've found it very useful, but I think that a lot of publishers think that it's about giving out information about books. To me, that just feels like advertising. Actually, nobody bothers with advertising online any more; nobody looks at it, because there are too many people trying to sell you stuff online. So to me, the use of social media is not so much about saying, "Here, buy my books," because I think people just tend to mute everybody who does that. It's about offering something that publishers can't offer. Really, the bottom line is it's about that connection between you and the public.

What sort of tweets get the best responses?

I tweet about all sorts of things. If you follow me, you'll find that I'll tweet articles, I'll tweet blog posts, and I'll tweet stories occasionally. I remember talking to Ian Rankin years ago when he just started on Twitter. I hadn't started and didn't really fancy the idea, because it seemed a bit too much like tweeting your bowel movements and that sort of thing. He said the way to use it is to use it as you would a cocktail party. You go and find the people who interest you and you talk to them about the things that interest you. You don't go up to somebody at a cocktail party and say, "Have you bought my book?" You genuinely give of yourself, and if you are yourself on there, then things will come of it. And things do come of it: for example, Ian met some of his TV and film contacts on Twitter, and I find that the same is true for me. You don't know what the result is going to be until you've done it. It's basically sending things out into the world and sometimes they'll bring something back and sometimes they won't.

For instance, I'm friends with another author who is on Twitter, but she doesn't tweet very much, and I said, "You really ought to get on here. I've met all these pretty interesting people." She's a very shrewd businesswoman, and she said, "Well, I understand that, but I resent anywhere where I have to write for free." I thought, 'That's an interesting way of putting it.' I see where she's coming from, but I also think she's wrong. You're not writing for free; you're sending out dandelion seeds into the world in the hope that they will take root. It's not time wasted. It's not procrastination, but you actually don't know what's going to come of it.

Let me give you some examples. I often tweet about my shed, which is where I work. After about six months of doing this – I would tweet about it every day and tell little stories about it – I got approached by Cuprinol and they said, "Would you mind designing and helping us build a celebrity shed? We'll pay you x amount of money and it will be auctioned for charity and put in this beauty spot around the British Isles." I thought, 'This is a very weird thing because it's a direct result of me tweeting about my shed!' Or you'll talk about your garden, and three days later, you'll get a call from a gardening programme saying, "Would you be on TV talking about your garden?" Or you will talk about a specific issue, and someone from a newspaper will call you up and say, "I hear you're interested in this. Can you contribute this?" So it's all about putting people together with other people and bonding them over things they're interested in. It works very well for me. I don't just say, "Buy my book."

What about Tumblr? Do you use that in a similar way?

I just started on that; I've not been going very long. Basically it's a nice way of linking longer pieces of text and blog posts and pictures. It's a slightly different demographic. I sense that Tumblr is more of a sort of young person's area, whereas Facebook has become incredibly corporate and dull, and Twitter is very much about writers and theatre people. There are sort of different tribes that migrate toward different types of social media, and some of them interest me and some of them don't. In some cases I like the format, and in some I don't. I like the format of Twitter and Tumblr, because it's not too limiting and you don't get adverts.

So it's about having a proper conversation with people who are interested in what you're interested in?

Exactly. It's also a medium in which people can follow me, but I don't have to follow everyone who follows me. That would, I think, be very unwieldy and tiresome and difficult. That's one of the things I find particularly wearing about Facebook is that everybody wants to be my friend, and I've never heard of any of them. I actually, frankly, don't *want* to know every detail of their lives, because I just don't want to know what 10,000 or 20,000 people are doing every day.

Do you find it very time-consuming? Do you set aside a regular time or just when you feel like it?

No, in the same way I wouldn't set aside a time to just to have a talk with somebody if I wanted to or if I was interested in them. I don't think of it in those terms. I think, in this position, you have to employ a kind doublethink because, obviously, you are doing it for your own purposes, but if you feel that you are doing it for business or promotional purposes, it won't work. You have to be doing it for another reason, and my reason is just that I happen to like it. It's a means of keeping in touch with people that I would like to see more often but I don't because we travel a lot. There are a lot of authors in this position. You know, we make friends, but we may meet each other in Dubai once a year or something. It would be quite nice to meet otherwise, but we just don't get a chance. The same goes for a lot of people from the stage that I've met. They keep in touch in that way because you work together with somebody and you form a bond, and then you don't see them again until you work together on some other stage, in some other show. Twitter particularly can help you keep in touch with people you wish you saw on a more regular basis, and of course there are readers who will chip in questions or comments. It is a nice way to interact where it doesn't take a very long time. You don't have to answer every question. If there are a lot of them, you can just ignore some of them, and if somebody is offensive, you can just block them and you'll never get to hear from them again. If only life were more like this!

How much time do you spend in an average week on social media?

I don't know. I don't count. I do what feels naturally right. It's a bit like saying, "How long do you spend eating?" It depends. You do it when you feel like it or when you have a little break. I don't tend to spend long periods of time. The nice thing about micro-blogging is that it really doesn't take long and it's for a very short attention span. So while I'm working, I may have Twitter open, and if I get a message I may stop and answer the message and then go back to it because it doesn't bother me. Or if I'm thinking about how to construct a phrase, and I haven't quite got it, I'll go on Twitter for two minutes and then when I come back, the thing will have consolidated in my mind and it'll be there. So it's kind of the equivalent of pacing up and down, I guess.

If you had to choose between a book launch in a bookshop or a virtual book tour, do you have a preference for one over the other?

It's a completely different animal. I don't think I can have a preference because they're so different. Different people come to different things. A certain kind of person will come to an event in a bookshop, whereas somebody else will contribute to an online event. Obviously, online tends to attract a different kind of audience, because a lot of them are in different countries and they wouldn't be able to just turn up to a local reading in Leeds or wherever. They both have their uses. They're very different. I generally think that the public doesn't think they're the same though, because some people have a need to actually meet you. Meeting you online isn't the same, and they would like their books signed or they would like to hear you read.

Do you get regular feedback from your publisher on the most effective forms of promotion whereby they say, "You did that and that worked really well and increased your book sales?"

Occasionally, yes. Usually you can tell what's going to increase book sales anyway, you don't need to ask. They will say something like, "Oh, Sainsbury's has taken x thousand" or "It's in so-and-so with three for two," and I know that this is a good thing. Beyond that, I don't look into the figures that much. Usually when something is just out, they'll give me the weekly sales figures. Other than that, I get sales figures once a year like everybody else, and they just get sent to the accountant and that's who deals with it. I can only be in one business at once, and I'm in the business of writing the things that somebody else will sell. What I can do to promote various stuff, I will do, but there are some aspects that I'm quite happy to have someone else in charge.

What is your favourite form of book promotion? What do you enjoy the most?

I enjoy festivals. I think it is nice to get out and meet other writers and meet the public, to express my appreciation to all the people who have helped sell the books and kept the books on the shelves. Festivals are nice because they generate excitement around reading and, worldwide, they're very popular. They have slightly different angles everywhere you go, and they're not always run in quite the same way, but it's an interesting way to do it. It generates a huge amount of interest in the book, particularly in smaller countries. I might go to somewhere like Estonia – just the fact of my being in the country at all and doing a festival, the book will just shoot into the Top Ten straight away. You can see an actual result there, which is nice. Obviously, tours and festivals take a lot of time, but I do think they work.

So basically you and your personality are important factors when it comes to book sales?

I think it's become that way with authors, generally. It's very difficult to get away from that truth. Most authors are quite shy, and it's sometimes an unpalatable truth to people to understand that a lot of the time, the book doesn't stand alone. Nobody will let it stand alone, because in a world where social media is prominent, they don't just want the books – they want to know about you. They want to hear from you, they want to connect with you directly, and they want to meet you, too. I know people who are really quite uncomfortable with this and who won't do it. A lot of people are uncomfortable with it, but they do it. Some people are perfectly fine with it, and it works for them.

If you had to give your top three tips for aspiring authors, what would they be?

For starters, I would say ditch the word 'aspiring'. Just write and don't worry much about the 'aspiring', because the only way to get good at something is by doing it; not by thinking that you like to do it or wanting to do it or wishing you can do it, but by just doing it. Everybody learns this way. It seems simple, but a lot of people are afraid to just do it. They're afraid they might not be ready or they might not be ready to show people or they're afraid of what to tell their friends. All of these things stand in the way of them doing it. So I think, probably, all my three points boil down to "just write."

The second one is "just read" as well. I'm horrified by the number of people who tell me grandiosely that they're writing a book, but they don't have time to do any reading! It seems absurd to me, because I don't understand how anybody can enter the literary world without having an interest in what other people are doing, as opposed to just what they're doing. I would say also, something we touched on when we first started talking: failure to get published or failure to have a wide readership or failure to make a lot of money doesn't make you a failure. A lot of people don't go into writing for the right reasons. They go into writing because they think it will help them make money or they would like to be famous. (Actually, I would say that most people have no idea what being famous is, or otherwise they wouldn't like it so much.) There is joy to be had in writing for its own sake. Not everybody who likes, say, tennis wants to be a pro, and as such, people should set themselves achievable goals in terms of their own personal growth and self-improvement, as opposed to wanting a glamorous lifestyle, which you don't get, or any of the other sort of illusory things that people feel they're going to get. You actually have to enjoy the process first.

So the third one is actually to enjoy what you do, because it may be the only benefit you get out of it, but if you do enjoy it, then it will be worth it.

SHARON LECHTER

"Successful books create an attachment to the emotions ... your heart gets involved."

Sharon Lechter is an American businesswoman best known as the co-author of the international bestseller *Rich Dad, Poor Dad.*

The book originally had no luck finding a publisher.

However, it went on to sell over 26 million copies in more than 100 countries, and became the cornerstone of a multi-million dollar publishing empire.

I've been involved in or have written 20 books in total, and every book has been slightly different. Overall, the initial idea is to sit back and ask: What is it you intend to accomplish? What is it that you want the reader to derive benefit from? What is your ultimate goal? Then, you look at it through the eyes of a reader. It's so important that a book tells a story. When you think of a textbook, it goes from your eyes to your *brain*. Successful books create an attachment to the *emotions*. They involve the emotions, so as you're reading it, your heart gets involved. So it's very important that you understand that you want to tell a story.

What is your end result? What do you want the reader to derive benefit from? Then you say: okay, a story has a beginning, a middle, and an end, so let's talk about what those three major components are. That's really the process that I use. Then I continue dividing it into subsets, until I get to the format of an outline. It's a very fluid outline that I can change if, while writing, something comes up that I think is important that's been left out. But I think it's really important to start with the end in mind and to tell a story and engage the emotions of the reader.

Do you speak your books or do you type them?

I type my books, but when I advise other writers I say you shouldn't – people get hung up in prepositional phrases and punctuation. You actually should write as you speak, so that as the reader is reading the book it's as if you're talking to them. The actual mechanical process I use is I type, but I type as I would speak.

How do you structure your writing week? When you're writing a book, do you write every single day for a predetermined number of hours, or do you set yourself a word count?

Well, I know quite a few people who say that that's how they do it. But no, I actually unplug and I do a deep dive: I'll literally spend three to six days in a row writing and absolutely immersing myself in the process, so that I'm living the process. For me to try and write for an hour a day just doesn't work for me. I will spend three to six days initially, and then I'll go away for about a month and do other things, and then I'll come back to it. That way, I can then see how I react to what I originally wrote and then improve upon it and continue.

At last count, you'd sold over 26 million copies of your books. What do you attribute that success to?

The numbers you're talking about are from the *Rich Dad* books that started my career in the personal development writing area. We did a lot of radio and television interviews, but I think the true success of the *Rich Dad* process is word of mouth. When you know that the book is going to move and inspire someone, they're going to tell everybody about it. When I meet people today and they tell me they've read *Rich Dad*, I always ask where they heard about it, and they'll say, "My mother told me," or "My brother told me." The element of true, long-term, lasting success is having a top quality book that impacts people in the way that they want to share it with other people. Obviously, PR is very important and it's a part of the process, but it's only one piece of the puzzle. A lot of people spend a lot of money on PR and don't see the results in sales. It's one portion of an overall strategy: you use social media; you use e-mail; you align yourself through association with other organisations. You get the right people to endorse your book, and by endorsing it you ask them to help you support it, so that you get that book in as many people's hands as possible. The next step is: how many of them will actually sit down and read those books;

and of those, will they be moved enough to say, "Wow, this is good," and tell other people about it?

You have used both self-publishing and mainstream publishing. Do you have any preference for either of the two?

The world of publishing has changed dramatically in the past ten years. And I follow that by saying the world of publishing has changed in the past two years. The world of publishing will change dramatically in the next year: because of the presence of online ordering ability and Amazon being a dot-com; because of the number of bookstores that are going out of business; and because of the rising popularity of e-books. All of those dynamics impact how to become a successful author and have multiple sales. You need to make sure your book is available in as many formats as possible. So from a standpoint of truly creating that success, it's important to have a strategy that incorporates all of that.

It used to be ten years ago that you needed to make sure you had a lot of shelf space, which meant you really needed to go with a mainline publisher, because they had that presence in the bookstores. This was true particularly if you only had one book, because very few people will pick you up if you only have a single title. In contrast to that, it's very important today to understand that that's not where the majority of the books are sold any more. In-store placement is important, but it's no longer the primary benefit of a mainstream publisher.

So, if you have a book and you already have a large network, it's very important that you give careful consideration to self-publishing. You need to balance your own network and the profitability of doing it on your own, versus having that ability to have a mainstream publisher to help you launch it. A mainstream publisher will do a very good job of helping you publicise your book for the first three weeks and then they move on to the next title. So, other than that initial launch, where you'll get great support from your publisher, you are the one driving the promotion of your book, and every author needs to recognise that. It's up to *you* to promote and continue the longevity of your product.

How much time do you devote to the promotion of your books? A lot of people think you write a book and that's 90 percent of the work finished.

Well, it goes in ebbs and flows. I promote any and every opportunity I get. When I finish today with you, I have an interview that's coming in from Australia that I'll be doing. So I always accept and try to pursue any opportunity to promote my books. When I'm writing a book, and then a book releases, I'm 180 percent into promotion of that book and doing very little writing. When I get a break because the book's up and running, I dive in and do some more writing. It's kind of an ebb and flow: you never stop promoting, and you never completely stop writing. Even in the promotion, you're writing blogs or articles to continue the promotion of your book. So the writing is something that's part of your everyday life.

You mentioned the kind of 'jigsaw' of promotion, that there are lots of different pieces to it. Is there a particular form of promotion that you've found effective when boosting book sales? Do you have a preference for online or offline?

Well, I think as we get more and more in this world of an online environment, it's so very important. You know, e-mail marketing that was very important a few years ago is not nearly as important as it used to be. I think you need to have that personal recommendation, so if you have someone who really believes in your work that has a large network, you're going to see a much stronger success from that person recommending your book to their network. I think you really want to look at those recommendations and testimonials that come together with them believing in your work and wanting to share it with their network – because that's going to be the most successful way. And get endorsements from organisations! You might get an opportunity to speak in front of an organisation. It's the power of association, which we talk about in my book, *Three Feet from Gold*. My last couple of books were with the Napoleon Hill Foundation – *Three Feet from Gold* and *Outwitting the Devil* – and the successes of those books are from constant, never-ending promotion and aligning ourselves with associations to help us promote them.

You also use social media – you touched on that earlier. Do you have any tips for using that to best effect?

As you're writing your book, come up with quotes or little quips along the way that can be used as tweets that can be put out on Twitter. Start building your Twitter following and your Facebook following and your LinkedIn following. Start building that discussion and getting people excited about your book by putting out little excerpts. That helps you build momentum before the release; and then after the release, have a strategy. You can sit down and pre-plan it so it's not something you have to do every day, but have a calendar of tweets that go out every single day that are tying back to your book. Have a Twitter account for the book, a Twitter account for yourself, and then have something on Facebook and LinkedIn as well, so that you can engender as much enthusiasm and as much recognition as you can.

It used to be that people said you have to contact someone three times to sell them something. Well, it's much more today and with today's mass media attack, sometimes it's ten or 12 times until people start recognising you, and by recognising you that gives immediate credibility. You just need to be out there everywhere you can, promoting your book and adding value. You want to give value to your audience.

One of the things that authors are telling me is that publishers are saying, "Don't go on a book tour; don't do festivals or signings – post something online instead." What do you think of that advice?

Well, book signings are less and less popular, and less and less effective. Again, a lot of that is because of the changes in the publishing world. We've built the success of the *Rich Dad* brand without book signings. If we had large events, we would do a book signing at the event. If I'm speaking at an event, I do a book signing there, but I don't necessarily arrange a bookstore signing unless they're coming after me and there's some opportunity for speaking so that you can market it and get the people into the bookstore. But it's very expensive to do a book tour, and today it's very popular to have radio and satellite tours where you stay in one location and you can reach stations all over the world. You really need to consider all the options before you become a road warrior and start spending a lot of money flying to cities to be on television, where you don't have the opportunity to also be in front of audiences.

How important do you think a book's title and cover are?

I call it the PIU factor: the Pick It Up factor. I think it's very important because, particularly in a bookstore or even on a social media platform, if you just see the book cover, you only have a couple of seconds for that book to hook you. For instance, *Think and Grow Rich*: that title is a hook and it's sold over 100 million copies. The hook is: *Think and Grow Rich* … well okay, how can I do that? With *Rich Dad, Poor Dad*, everybody related. You either have a rich dad or a poor dad; or if you're a man you say, "I am one or the other." So it's very important that people have a title that's going to mean something and make somebody want to pick it up, and when they pick it up then they're going to say, "I want to buy this." Particularly if you're in a bookstore, you're in a sea of a lot of different books, so your cover design needs to be eye-catching, and your title needs to be something that makes them say, "Okay, I want to see what that means."

In the early days, with your first book in the *Rich Dad* series, it was rejected and you couldn't find a publisher to take it up, so you self-published. Tell me more about that.

We actually published it through a company called Tech Press, which is a publishing company that my husband and I own. So it was technically not self-published, but it was turned down. One of the things that we did through persistence is that we continued promoting it and continued sharing the message. Within three years, not only had we gotten it to the bestseller list on our own, but that's when all the major publishing houses came to us. So it put us in a much stronger bargaining position in order to allow a big publisher to step in, and it was at a point in time when we really needed a big publisher because we were having a hard time getting the shelf space and meeting the demand. But understand, that was again in 1997, so bookstore shelves and placement were very important. It's still very important today that you have your book in bookstores and have placement if it's a title that you think is going to be available and interesting to the general public. So you have to look at all the factors – they just weigh differently than they did five or ten years ago.

You mentioned that it took you three years. A lot of aspiring authors give up after six or 12 rejections. What gave you the determination and faith to keep going?

Well, we did have immediate success; we just didn't have a publisher. We continued publishing it through our company, Tech Press. Our first print run was 1,000 books, then our next print run was 5,000, then 10,000, then 50,000. We were blessed with success from the very beginning as far as popularity of the book, but it was a lot of hard work because we did it all on our own. That persistence in respect of persistently promoting is what an author needs to do. You need to persistently promote. So many authors go into it thinking, 'I'm going to write it and I'm going to put it out there,' it's kind of like, 'Build it and people will come.' That's a real fallacy. Particularly in this world of so much competition and new media, and so many new books being written, in order to sell your book you must be persistent in promotion. You must be constantly building your network, and knowing that one e-mail out isn't going to cut it. You're going to have to repeatedly reach out and tell people about the book, continue updating and getting people to post reviews on Amazon, continue to get people to have it ever-present in their minds. If you want to be successful, it's up to you to be driving the promotion, never-ending.

The *Chicken Soup for the Soul* series, they had lots of rejections. Napoleon Hill's *Think and Grow Rich* had rejections. A lot of the most successful authors on earth had a lot of rejections before they got accepted. It comes back to: how many no's can you take before you get to that yes? That's the art of having faith, and that's where that faith is so important. You have faith in yourself and you have faith in your book.

How important to you is reader feedback? Do you try out your ideas to get a feel for the topics that are really striking a chord?

Well, I think reader feedback is very important, but I guess it is more *consumer* feedback, (because when you write the book, the feedback is important at that point too, but you've already written it). For instance, I'm working on *Think and Grow Rich for Women* and it will be published next year, but I'm out there talking to people about it right now. I'm getting people to tell me what they think about *Think and Grow Rich* and how they use it in their own success, so that I'm getting the understanding of that concept through other people's eyes. So I'm not just saying it from my perspective, but I'm getting as many perspectives as possible. It is also very important to do your research and make sure you know that what you are sharing is true and accurate. Today, so many things are on the Internet that you accept as truth and you can get caught up, so you really need to do your research and make sure that the information you're sharing is accurate.

You're an incredibly successful businesswoman, but as a writer what would you say your challenges and frustrations are? Do you find it easy to write books?

Probably the number one challenge for me is time and focus: because I'm running a business, I'm running a financial education business for young people, I'm writing, *and* I'm promoting. So time is a big issue for me, and finding six days where I can concentrate on my writing is something that I have to literally carve into my calendar. My biggest challenge is having enough days in the week and enough hours in the day to accomplish what I want to accomplish.

If you could go back to revisit Sharon Lechter of 20 or 30 years ago, what advice would you give her with the knowledge you have now?

We all learn through experience. I think 20 years ago I would have probably made myself a little more aware of the importance that writing was going to play in my future. Actually, 20 years, gosh, that wasn't so long ago. I was already involved in publishing; I helped start the children's talking books industry, so no, I already knew I was into writing 20 years ago.

Twenty-one years ago was when I really dedicated myself to financial education and financial literacy. At that point in time, I would have liked to have known the importance of bringing people together, the importance of the mastermind, the importance of the networking, and the power of association. We learned that because that's what created our success, and if I'd known that from the beginning, we could've reached so many more people, so much more quickly.

Children's financial literacy is one of your big passions. What would you say is the difference between writing something that has an impact on children and writing something that has an impact on adults?

The process is the same. But when you write for children, you need to put yourself in the mind-set of the age group you're writing for, to make sure that you're not speaking down to them. So many things for kids are like a tutorial, telling kids what to do. What I spend my time on is creating books and programmes and products that ignite the entrepreneurial knowledge in a child: the entrepreneurial spirit, and the thirst for learning, that allows them to discover new things. To experience the wealth of knowledge available to them as it relates to money, as it relates to time management. Everything I create for them is something that allows them to discover knowledge. It's not a tutorial, it's not a dictatorial. It's a discovery platform.

JAMES REDFIELD

"I travelled all over the US and I stopped in little shops and gave 1,500 copies away ..."

James Redfield is best known for writing *The Celestine Prophecy*, a novel exploring the narrator's spiritual awakening.

Redfield originally self-published the book – selling 100,000 copies – before Warner Books agreed to publish it.

The book has since sold over 23 million copies, and spent 165 weeks on the *New York Times* bestseller list.

The book's concept has been expanded into a series of three sequels. A film adaptation of the book was made in 2006.

I was a psychotherapist: in the course of my work I was very interested in the broad range of spiritual theory and religious thought across all religions. I was very interested in the direct experience of spirituality – as opposed to doctrines and theologies. So, focusing on the 'experience' really got me in touch with a lot of popular expressions. This was the late '80s, and in academia there was a lot of theory about the human potential, which was essentially our potential to exhibit a greater, more fully functioning, psychological place. I was interested in it psychologically but also from a spiritual point of view, in terms of what the human culture was experiencing in the area of spirituality.

So with all of that going on, I attempted to write an academic book, which was more spiritual psychology. You know: what is human spiritual potential? What are the experiences? But it just did not resonate with me. I thought I had some good ideas, and I thought I had my finger on what was actually happening in the wider conversation, especially in the United States, which sort of came into the current kind of New Age thought and movement that was happening in the US, Europe and elsewhere. But taking the academic approach just didn't feel impactful enough.

So I thought what I would do was just write a novel about those experiences and what people were discovering. I was very much into hidden knowledge about spirituality, and the whole idea of old manuscripts and the Dead Sea Scrolls had just come out. So I just crafted a novel based on a lot of my own experiences, but also trying to describe this richness of spiritual experience that I felt was emerging within human culture. So I wrote that book and that was *The Celestine Prophecy*. As you know, it took off and was very much a pass-along book, not just within the US but also outside the US.

I actually created my own publishing company to publish the book, just because I wanted to get it out more rapidly. Of course, it became a pass-along book all around the world, and finally I turned it over to a larger publisher.

That's what got me going. What happened was that I was able to craft a story that spoke to people, especially in the area of synchronicity or meaningful coincidences that happen in our lives. What you get is evidence that there's a richer experience, there's a spiritual kind of built-in programme in the universe so that we are helped to manifest our greatest contribution. That was the first book, and it became this worldwide pass-along book. I think it was in '96 or '97 – it was the number-one bestselling book in the whole world. It surprised me as much as anybody else!

It spent 165 weeks on the *New York Times* bestseller list and sold more than 23 million copies. What do you think was the appeal of that book? What was it that made the difference compared to other similar New Age or spiritual books?

I think it pointed to direct experiences that people were already having and didn't know how to understand. I think *The Celestine Prophecy*, with its clarity about the psychology of spirituality – how we get in our own way, how we can cultivate this greater experience if we pursue it in a certain way – all these things are clarifying for people.

It's interesting because as I wrote it, it was a clarification for me as well. This awakening was happening around the world at the same time, and this book I believe just put it into words for people. They could see that it was relevant to their own experience.

You self-published your book first before it attracted the notice of Warner Books. It's widely rumoured that you sold your first 100,000 copies out of the trunk of your car. Is that correct?

That's the mythology, but I never sold a single book out of my trunk. [*Laughs*] What I did instead was I gave them away! This is something that I thought out very carefully. I believe that you get back an amplified amount of energy from what you give. I just travelled around with the book. I think the first printing was 2,000 copies, so I took maybe 1,500 of those and I just travelled around to local bookshops. I had a good distributor – New Leaf, out of Atlanta – so it was very easy for the bookstores to order it. I was fortunate in getting that distributor.

So I just walked in and said, "Here's the book and I'm the author." I talked to the owner or the buyer, saying, "Here's a book and I'd love for you to read it. I think it's something your readers and consumers would love to read. Here's how you can order it if you want more copies."

But then I did something else. I gave everyone who happened to be in the bookshop a copy. Synchronicity being the operating principle, I thought it was appropriate. I just figured: if they're there when I walk in, it means they're there to read this book, so that's what I did. So I travelled all over the US and I stopped in little shops and gave 1,500 copies away. It just started to become a pass-along phenomenon immediately: it was quadrupling every week in sales. So that was a big cash-flow problem initially, but it was a good problem to have. We just kept printing books and I think by the time the new Warner version came out, we had sold about 140,000 copies, which was only after about nine months.

That's a wonderful achievement! Did you have any mentors at that time, or any strategy or a marketing plan?

I read a couple of books on self-publishing. I created a company called Satori Publishing. We did it pretty much the way any small publisher would do it. We went to the shows, sent e-mails out, and all that sort of thing.

With that kind of growth, it was funny with the cash flow. You get paid from the bookstores about three months after they sell the book. Really, it's the distributor paying me, and the stores pay the distributor in three months, so it can take about five months to get any money back from the distributor. So we were about five months behind the curve. We had to just keep coming up with initial capital to buy more books, to keep the pipeline going. That was a good problem to have. We were able to secure all those funds.

As soon as it was breaking even, profits and book sales were more than adequate to keep the supply going. I thought, 'We're just going to do this and I don't need another publisher now.' But I talked to Warner Publishing, and Larry Kirshbaum was president at that time. I also had two or three other publishers saying, "Sorry we didn't return your calls before, but we want to talk to you now!" But Larry Kirshbaum was certainly the most knowledgeable, and I liked what his strategy would be to sort of start all over and do the hardcover first, and then take it worldwide. I thought he had an interesting plan. So it allowed me to keep writing, and by that time, there were calls for lectures all over the world. It allowed for me to travel much more broadly than I would've been able to otherwise.

This is something that many authors find as they become more successful. There are only 40 to 60 hours in a working week, so you need better ways to leverage your time. What are the most effective promotion methods you've found to reach readers?

It was communication with the bookstores and the churches, and the more alternative churches. We really went with Unity churches and Science of Mind churches and other more traditional denominations, because they were hosting a lot of the lectures, but all that is over now. The big chain stores have put all the mom-and-pop bookstores out of operation … we've got all these big chains and not so many mom-and-pop operations, so it's much harder now.

A young writer has to somehow reproduce that buzz phenomenon with a book. They try to do e-mails, events, online events and so on. But to me, it's a matter of: *don't finish a book until it's a pass-along book. Don't publish it until it's done. Keep working until you get a book that's a pass-along that somebody wants to give to their friends, to share that information.* That in itself is difficult now. Baby boomers just read like crazy, but millennials don't. They get their information from the Internet and short blog snippets. Their perception is that there's so much information out there, they don't have time to read a book. So that's a lot harder for someone who is writing a book. But again, the competition was also fierce when *The Celestine Prophecy* came out, and the only difference for me was that I took as long as I needed to finish the book.

It was probably a five-year process in the writing of it. But my goal was that I just wanted to be clear and I wanted to be interesting. I really spent a lot of time doing that. I really felt like I was driven to just be as clear and helpful as possible, so I took an extra year. I actually finished it, I thought, and I just left it and put it away for about six months, and then went back and got it out and rewrote it a last time. It was night and day. It was so clear where I had over-written passages, and some passages had become boring, and others were too short and needed to be elaborated on.

Looking back, I realise that there was a kind of spirit about that book. When I was doing that final revision, I had these mystical experiences where the room just kind of lit up. I obviously had help with that book that you would have to say was quite mystical in nature. But my message to other writers is: don't think you're finished until you can put it away where you can't remember it, and you have to read it as a reader would. That's the key thing.

The other part was that I tested it. I made about 20 copies and gave it to friends of friends, people who had no obligation towards me to say anything positive. I would have them read it and then make a note any time they got to a place that was not clear or that they got lost. I did that for about four months, I guess. What came out of it was that I was able to get it as clear for the readers as possible.

I have a lot of people asking me, "What can I do to get my book out?" and that's exactly what I tell them. Make sure it's complete! Just because you understand it or think you do, don't take that as meaning that other people will understand it. Keep working on it until somebody says, "Can I have an extra copy to send to a friend of mine?" Those are the words you want to hear when you give people copies to read. From testing, I really knew that the book would be fairly well received. But I had no idea that there would be so much excitement about it.

You hold webinars each month, don't you, to stay in touch with your readers? How easy did you find that as a transition? A lot of authors might feel a bit techno-phobic when they first start using the Internet, because it all feels so new.

We try to make it easy on our side, where you just have to push a button or two. It's a Global Prayer Project; it's an organisation that comes together to help the world through their spiritual energy. That really makes it easier because it's people coming together to help the world and I certainly keep in touch with them that way. I get to talk 15 minutes every other week. So we have around 40-50,000 people around the world come together for these things and everybody who signs up is committing to either be hooked up with us on Skype or the Internet or the phone lines, when we're holding this one-hour prayer session.

You also use Facebook and Twitter and a blog. Do you have any tips for using those? Obviously you don't want to go on there and just say, "Read my book," you want to be sharing ideas.

Yeah, and it's easier with spirituality because people inherently want to explore and develop that in themselves. *The Twelfth Insight* was the fourth book in the *Celestine* series. Remember, each book covered certain insights that I was describing as social phenomena, I wasn't making this stuff up. I was reporting what people were concluding about their spirituality. So once I got to 12, I was waiting to report a new insight.

Some of these books were six or seven years apart, but I could say, "Hey, there's new insight afoot out there." *The Twelfth Insight* conclusion, of course, is that we are learning how to cultivate it. In other words, there are just

12 awakenings about the culture; all of the information is out there, and all we have to do is cultivate it from that knowledge and we can have a deep experience of living spiritual lives that really is more miraculous than anybody ever thought. That was the *Twelfth Insight*, and now what's left is to cultivate it and live it.

My advice to writers in reaching out to people that way is to give them something they can do. Give them something: a shift they can make in their lives; information they can use because it helps them in their lives. Because my other *Twelfth Insight* thesis is that the activation for the spiritual life happens in giving. So we have to give to the other people we meet in our lives, and what you have to give is information or a testimony or whatever it is. You give them what's working for you and that becomes a synchronicity for them, somebody arriving with the information at just the right time. What happens when we seek to help somebody is it opens an intuitive spiritual channel in our own lives, because you have to ask, "What can I say to this person?" That opens up into answers of what to say to a given person, how to be helpful to them, and how to be a synchronicity to them.

When we manipulate people – when we do what's best for us instead of thinking what's best for them – when we think what do we get from people instead of what can we give, that's bad karma. The karmic structure in this world is: if you are honestly helpful to people and seek to open up and find your intuitive guidance in order to do that, then your karma shifts in such a way that you attract more people to arrive at just the right time to help you in this world. That's the solution to *everything*. Every problem – economically, financially, in relationships – that's how miraculous solutions come, always through other people who come into our lives who give us information or direct help. That's what this world was designed to be and to become. That's pretty exciting, so I get all excited going around talking about this.

So that's what I do. And I still write, you know. The last book took number nineteen on the *New York Times* bestseller list. That's pretty good considering the detailed information I was giving, I thought, and it was published in about 20 countries. So I'm still pretty hopeful that people out there, in spite of how bad it looks and how corrupt it is, are getting it in terms of this new spirituality that's directly available within our own experience.

How many of your books are sold as e-books compared to physical books nowadays?

I think it's a greater percentage with every book. This last one was probably 25 percent or more.

Do you think there's something special that comes across in sharing a book compared to speaking to people? Obviously you're sharing your ideas all the time when you're speaking or doing radio interviews. Is there something special about sharing your message in print?

I definitely think everybody should have a book if they have a message. If you've got a message, it's important to get it out, and I think we all do. I think that's the way it works. The most important place is with the direct people that synchronistically cross our paths. This is all orchestrated. It's a spiritual dynamic built into the universe. You can bet that anybody you chance to have a conversation with, or you meet, or you walk into a restaurant at the same time through a door; that's all orchestrated. That's an orbiting of people who need to speak to each other, which is one of the main things, of course, throughout all my books.

We're having a great transition out there. This materialistic idea of, "Oh, everything's a chance event, nothing's meaningful," that some people hold onto because they think it's less scary or something; it's all falling apart. The financial crash was because of bad karma coming from our behaviour toward each other. You can't survive in this world materialistically any more. You can't just use your logic, because everything's falling apart. Logical habits don't work any more. Logic is important, but logic that comes from an intuitive source is what you want. You want to be checking out your intuitions and you've got to find your guidance, but guidance is within. You can cultivate that just by trying to be helpful. It all builds on itself and pretty soon you're living in what I call "the miracle universe", instead of this material illusion. There was always illusion; it was necessary to be able to name everything and get the laws down and create all the institutions and everything. Well they're corrupt, every one of them, but we've created all these institutions to help people, and now we just have to clean them up. That's going to have to come from a spiritual point of view and spiritual living.

Do you have plans for another book, or are you writing another one at the moment?

I'm writing another one that is much more about the culture we live in and how we can reform it spiritually, and the consciousness from which we can reform and make the world better. We have to focus on the grassroots transformation, rather than anything that can possibly happen from the top down.

Do you expect that will take you five years to write?

I sure hope not! [*Laughs*] The writing process for me is interesting because it's not given in any kind of completed form. It's given in visions. My experience of writing is that I get the impulse or intuition of what needs to be said, and it always has a beginning and an ending, no matter what kind of book it is. I'll get the beginning and some of the major themes of the book and an ending. Then I try to, in short little outlined statements, start at the beginning and go through the whole book. All I do is sit in front of a blank sheet of paper and I'll start writing things. Then, I go through and, without being too strictly regimented by my outline, I just go ahead and start writing.

This is not a novel; I'm starting a new genre for myself. This is written much the way I'm talking to you: it's direct and I try to really talk about the times we live in and what affects every one of us. I try to be really direct with the reader in a straightforward book. It'll have adventure in it because my life is pretty adventurous, but I'm going to confront the conspiracy theorists in a helpful, spirited kind of way. Just again, for clarity for people, for what needs to happen: how do you live in a world that's as distrustful as this one, and how do we build something new and better?

BERNARD CORNWELL

"Something has to happen on every page ... you cannot bore people."

Bernard Cornwell, OBE, has been a bestselling author for over 30 years.

He has written over 50 books including: the *Sharpe* series, about Napoleonic Wars rifleman Richard Sharpe, which was adapted for a TV series; *The Warlord Trilogy* (1995-1997); *The Grail Quest Series* (2000-2003); and *The Saxon Series* (2004-2010).

His books have sold over 20 million copies worldwide.

Bernard was born in London, raised in Essex, and now lives in Massachusetts with his wife.

How did I start writing books? It was insane! I used to have a proper job. I was head of current affairs television at the BBC in Northern Ireland, where two of my reporters were Jeremy Paxman, who can't have been more than 22, and Gavin Esler. We were making a film of an event when the Northern Irish Tourist Board invited a group of American travel agents to Ulster. Ulster as a tourist destination! This was plainly insanity. Judy came out of a lift at the hotel at the event, and I took one look at her and said, "I'm going to marry that one." And reader, I did.

The trouble was, she couldn't live in Britain for very good family reasons, and I had no ties, so we moved to the United States. The American government wouldn't give me a green card, so I airily said, "I'll write a book, darling," and I did. And that was about 34 years ago. I just went to the States and wrote a book. It was *completely* insane! [*Laughs*] And it's been going on ever since. We're still married and I'm still writing.

What gave you the confidence to do that? The first literary agent you approached rejected your book, but that was followed by a seven-book deal with HarperCollins! That was quite a big chunk to bite off.

Yeah, and I'm not sure it would happen today. You know better than I do that the publishing world is in turmoil. The first literary agent turned me down, and then I sent the book to, I think it was Heinemann, and Heinemann accepted the book and offered me a reasonable advance. I knew the advance was not going to keep me to write a second book, and I just didn't know what to do.

We were invited to a Thanksgiving Day party in New York to watch the Macy's Parade, and I was standing on a balcony, and the McDonald's All-American high school band was high-stepping under me, playing selections from *Oklahoma* or something, and a voice behind me said, "They do this sort of thing frightfully well, don't they?" Needing a break in conversation, I said, "Oh, you're English!" "Yes," he said. "What do you do?" I asked, and he replied, "I'm a literary agent." I said, "Oh, I've just written a novel," whereupon he turned around, and walked away.

I followed him through the crowd, got him again, and continued, "I had an offer on my novel," at which point his eyes lit up, and he asked, "How much?" I replied, "Three thousand pounds, world rights." Then he said, "It must be a fucking awful novel," and walked away again! So I grabbed him a third time, "Please … grovel, grovel … read my novel!" "Oh, if I must, I suppose so. Meet me at the oyster bar."

So I dragged him to the oyster bar and took the novel with me. He phoned me that evening and said, "How much money do you want for it?" I had absolutely no idea what to say. I can't remember the figure I said, but it was probably pretty low, like £12,000 or £15,000, and within two or three days he had it. He had the seven-book deal. And he's still my agent!

So what gave you the confidence and the tenacity to keep after him when he was saying "no"?

Desperation, absolute desperation! I was in a situation where I had literally burned my boat. I couldn't go back to Britain. Well, I could've gone back to Britain and gotten a job. I was in the States, I was with Judy and we weren't married then. I simply needed enough money to stay and pay the rent and crawl through another year while I wrote another book. It was just sheer desperation. He seemed heaven sent. Your head is wondering whether you're going to sign a bad deal, and you meet someone who's in the business.

Are you motivated by deadlines? How did you cope with a seven-book deal?

I've never worried about a deadline, ever, and, I don't think I've ever missed one. Oh gosh, there's so much to say about this one! Where to begin? It helps to have been a journalist. You're not frightened of the empty page. So I never had any great worries about actually sitting down and putting the stuff on paper. The confidence, you're asking about, I don't think I was confident at all! It was all desperation.

There's also the fact that what I'm doing is not difficult. A friend of mine is Sebastian Faulks [author of *Birdsong*], and what Sebastian does *is* difficult: he's shooting at a very small target a very long way away, and even a near-miss is incredibly interesting and brilliant. It's wonderful. I'm shooting at a barn door from five paces with a shotgun. I have absolutely no excuses.

That's a nice metaphor. So what sort of challenges would you say you have with your books when you're writing, and how do you overcome them? Or even when you're publicising your books?

Oh, publicising is much worse than writing it. Well, always the big challenge is the plot, always. I mean, why do my books work – which I assume they do? My theory is that they work because I'm a storyteller, and people want to find out what happens. Finding out what happens is what drives people through the book and brings them back for more books, and that's the most difficult bit.

I've just finished a book and it probably took the better part of five months to do the first draft. The second and third drafts take two days each, or three days, or four days, or five days. Because the difficult thing is simply getting the story right, and the mechanics of the plot have to be hidden. The reader must never see the way they're being manipulated. That's the difficult bit. That said, it's still a barn door at five paces.

So how much time do you spend planning your books?

I don't: I can't. I wish I could. You know I really envy people like Joanne Rowling, who plotted out all seven *Harry Potters*. C.S. Forester [author of the *Hornblower* books] did the same thing, he had the whole book down, and Patrick Robinson [*New York Times* bestselling author of suspense thrillers], who I talked to a couple of years back, does the same. He has the whole book in note form and just goes away and writes it. I just can't do it! For me, the joy of writing is the same as the joy of reading: to find out what happens. I start with a situation, throw the hero or heroine into that situation, write that first chapter, and I genuinely don't know what's going to happen in the second. I know where I want the book to go, I have a destination in mind, but I have no idea how I'm going to get there. Really, until you get to about three-quarters of the way through, you don't see how you're going to get there. If a publisher wanted a synopsis in advance, I would never have been published.

All the more incredible that you managed to get a seven-book deal with Harper! They must've been very confident.

That was Susan Watt, who is still there and is a lovely and amazing woman. I'm a rare author: after 30 years, I have the same wife, same publisher, and the same agent. Susan told me right at the beginning, "It's going to take four or five books to make you into a bestseller," and I think it was the fifth book. There are all sorts of theories about that. Women are wonderfully adventurous readers. A woman will go into a bookshop and browse, and will take a chance on an author she's never heard of. Men are incredibly dull and boring. They'll look at a book and say, "Well, I've never heard him," and they'll wait until they see three or four titles, which proves the guy can write. I have an enormous number of women readers, which is lovely. There were some fairly gruesome covers with soldiers killing each other. Not exactly 'chick lit'!

It's been said that you write some of the best battle scenes of any writer, past or present. What would you say are the essential ingredients, or building blocks, for writing a battle scene?

Well, I read the wonderful John Keegan's book, *The Face of Battle*, years ago, and it really revolutionised military history. What he was saying was that you can't just be cold-blooded and say, "The fourth division moved up two miles, and the third corps did this." He asked what was it actually like? What are they seeing, smelling, hearing, and doing? Basically, I put myself in the position of the narrator or the hero, and just think, 'What is he actually smelling at this moment? What is he seeing?' You keep on changing the point of view and zipping off and getting a wide shot. [*Laughs*]

I don't know how I do it! I'm rewriting the last chapter for the new book and it's all battle and it's great fun! That's also the key to it. It's got to be fun. You know, I get bored to death with people saying, "Oh, writer's block!" and "Isn't this hard?" For God's sake, we all volunteered for this job! No one put a gun to my head and said, "I'm sorry about this, but you're going to have to stop being a television producer and you're doomed to be a writer!" "Oh no, no, please – anything but!" I mean, come on, people would give their eyeteeth to do what I do, and then people bitch about it? It's great fun; I love it.

With historical fiction, you're blending real events and real characters with imaginary heroes. How much poetic licence do you think a writer should have when dealing with historical fact, and where do you draw the line?

I draw the line at making them up. I think most historical novels, probably 99 percent of them, have a big story and a little story. The big story in *Gone with the Wind* is: will the south win the Civil War. The little story is: can Scarlett save Tara? The trick is to flip them, so you put the big story in the background and the little story in the foreground. I don't reinvent history. Where I do change events, and you do have to, I put a historical note on the back that says: look, this didn't actually happen this way and this is what really happened. I don't know what the line is.

In the new book, there's a battle at Tettenhall in the year 910 AD, and the two Danes who died, the leaders, are called Healfdan and Eowils. I used two characters from previous books and just changed the names. I'm sure a few purists will say, "Oh you idiot, everyone knows it was Healfdan who did that." Well, you know I couldn't give a bugger. But, I couldn't do that with the Battle of Waterloo, because everyone knows about Waterloo. You can't simply say, "Well, I don't want to use the name Wellington because I used Joe Bloggs in a previous book so it's Joe

Bloggs instead." That wouldn't work. So you must confess your 'sins' always!

Your characters have all got some elements of light and dark in them. Is it important, do you think, for characters to have flaws in them?

Yeah, I mean, we're all flawed. Well, you may not be, but I am. They're slightly more interesting. I really don't think about it; I just write them. Uhtred, the one I'm writing about at the moment, I'm making him even more flawed. People seem to like his flaws, so I'm sort of exaggerating them in the new book.

You were a TV producer before you became a well-known author. How did you cope with the transition to being on the receiving end of the media? Did you find that strange?

No, not really. I think I've always wanted to be a writer, right from the get-go. When I was a teenager, I had this idea that writing was better than working. Also, I think television is a young man's game. I left when I was 36 or 37, and that was probably the time to leave, unless you want to go on to become an executive and spend your life having power lunches. Having worked in the business, I was never frightened of going into a studio. If you wanted to use one word to describe me, I'm sure it would be 'glib'. Sit me down in front of an interviewer and I'm fine, I don't even think about it.

So your previous job took away some of the mystique of the media? Some authors feel very intimidated being interviewed.

Well, it does help. I did a promotional video for a book called *The Fort*, and the American publisher set it up and they said, "This is what we're doing and we're going to need four days of your time up in Maine." I looked at what they were doing and I said, "No you won't, you'll need me for one afternoon," and they just refused to believe me. But we started at 11 o'clock in the morning and we were over by half past four. I knew what they were doing and I knew what they wanted. They assumed, I'm sure, that I was like most authors: tongue-tied in front of a camera. Cameras just don't scare me.

You mentioned your promotional video. What other forms of promotion do you use?

This is tough. The thing about a book tour, say, is that if you need to do a book tour, it's not going to work. If you don't need to do a book tour, it works brilliantly. I remember when I began and HarperCollins would send me off around Britain to sign books, and, you know, two men and a dog would turn up, if you were lucky. You needed to do it and it just didn't work.

I refuse to do book tours in the USA, because book tours in America are just hell on wheels. [*Laughs*] Oh yes, fucking terrible. So I just say a straight "no" to it. Most years, I do a tour in Britain, which I enjoy. I love meeting the readers! You get ideas from them; you have to listen to them. The book I've just written, a chunk of it came from what people have said to me, what they liked and disliked about the other books.

So it's important for you to listen to feedback? On your website, you have a lot of questions from readers, and you respond to all of those as well?

Well, I'll be honest, my lovely assistant, Cece, answers the ones she can answer. I say to her, "Think nasty thoughts so you sound like me." [*Laughs*] She passes on the ones she can't answer. So they all do get answered.

What about other social media? Do you have a blog or do you tweet?

I'm on Facebook. About a month ago, Facebook closed my page down – absolutely no explanation whatsoever. I finally managed to get an answer from them, and they said the page was being abused, which it wasn't. It was complete idiocy, and you cannot get in touch with them. I think the answer I got was an automatic answer. So finally I wrote a snail mail to the CEO, and said, "What on earth is going on?" It came back the day she got the letter – very weird.

And they reinstated it?

They did. I still don't have an explanation. I assume the reinstatement meant they realised they were wrong.

How many followers do you have on Facebook?

God, it's thousands. It's a fan page, and there are actually two because HarperCollins runs one as well and I think that's got even more. There's one that's supposed to be my personal one, which the last time I looked had got about 5,000.

Is that your preferred form of social media or Internet marketing?

I think my preferred form is probably my own website, simply because that's where the questions tend to come. I do get quite a lot of questions on Facebook, but I steer them onto my website.

How many questions do you get per week or per month?

At least 50 per week.

You think that's one of the best ways to keep your readers engaged?

I think the best way to keep my readers engaged is to give them a new book every year. I'm sure this is true of almost all bestselling authors, at least storytellers like me: the way to kill your market is to die. [*Laughs*] Think about it! When I was a little boy, Alistair MacLean [author of *The Guns of Navarone*] was huge, but who reads Alistair MacLean now? You have to keep priming the pump.

I remember saying to Judy years and years ago, back when I was young so I knew everything, and I hadn't even written halfway through the first book: "There are two ways to do this: one is to run a marathon, the other is to be a sprinter. I'm a marathon runner." I didn't expect the first book to burst on the world like *Harry Potter* did. I'm full of envy for those people who can be sprinters, but so many of them burn out. I'm a marathon runner, and I have 50 books in print and they *are* in print and still selling. Every time you bring out a new one, it spurs sales for the backlist.

Publishing has changed dramatically over your career as a writer, as a result of the Internet and digital publishing. Do you think of these changes as a good thing?

I guess I'm neutral. I read on an iPad, and Judy on a Kindle. I don't know whether it's good or bad. A fish doesn't complain about the sea it swims in. I don't know where it's going. One part of me thinks I'm awfully glad that I had my career before e-books came in. But another part of me thinks you probably sell more e-books at a slightly lower price than you do of physical books. In the end, what I do is I produce a story and it is up to the publisher how that story reaches the public.

My big worry is when somebody manages to break the code. Already, if you go online – and you'll find this with every author you're interviewing – there must be 20 or 30 sites that are offering my books at a dollar or one pound each. What they've done is, some guy has sat there and scanned the whole book and they're selling a PDF edition. They're all over the damn place!

They try to take them down if they can. I know that all the publishers get together and hire someone, or a company, that scours the Internet to find these people. I'm not too worried about the PDF, because who wants to read a whole book in a PDF version? It's going to be really a pretty gruesome experience. But eventually someone's going to crack the code and the books will be out there. Look what happened to the music industry. File sharing could kill us, but I don't know enough about it to talk about the technicalities.

Do you know the percentage of your physical books compared to your e-books that are sold?

It is changing all the time. I think it is over 60 percent e-books now being sold in the American market. I don't know in the British market, but maybe my agent would know. I get reams of paper, which are covered with figures that I don't look at. It could be hidden in there somewhere.

So you don't check on your sales figures then?

No, I genuinely don't. I don't read reviews either. I trust my publisher. I trust my agent. If I believed in God, I would fall to my knees daily and thank him for my life. So no, I don't check.

How do you see yourself? As a writer; as a speaker; as a marketer; as a thought leader; as a storyteller? Or all of those?

I'm a storyteller. I am a writer; I'm not going to deny it. The trouble with writers is, it covers this huge spectrum. At one end, you've got these incredibly clever people: Annie Proulx [author of *The Shipping News*] and Barbara Kingsolver [author of *The Poisonwood Bible*], and people who are telling us about ourselves, and revealing human dilemmas and truths. At the other end, you've got people like me who are just telling a story.

Telling a story is instinctive for me. I don't have to think about the mechanics of it, in which case I'm very lucky. But you still have to write it. The great P.G. Wodehouse, when he finished a page in the typewriter, would pin it to the wall of his room and if he wasn't happy with the page it went very low down. If he was happy it went high up, or somewhere in between, so that when he looked around the room he could see which pages needed work. I love that story. Something has to happen on every page, there's got to be something that catches the reader's eye. In other words, you cannot bore people.

I seem to recall that you write 6,000 words on a good day. What is a typical writing day like for you?

I certainly used to, but I've slowed down. I'm getting old and decrepit now. Well, I used to write two books a year. I stopped doing that because about eight years ago, I said, "I'm an actor," so I spent my summer on stage in a summer stock theatre, which is like a rep theatre. So basically the theatre took out the time for the second book, which gives me more time to do the one. I can probably churn out 5,000 or 6,000 words if I had to, but I don't. My typical day is: I start early, I'm usually at work by about six o'clock in the morning, and then there's lots of breaks in the day to walk the dog and have lunch.

Do you have a regimented day when you're writing? Or is it more random than that?

You can't force it. Certainly when you're writing the first draft, there are whole days where you're probably playing Solitaire instead of writing, or flipping through the websites to find out what's happening in the world. If a book starts to go really, really slowly like that, I know that there's actually something wrong. But you can't force it; I used to try and force it, but it didn't work. You simply have to wait for it to sort itself out, which it will.

I spend my life doing what I call "putting doors in alleyways" in every single book I've ever written. I'll use *Sharpe* as an example. Say Sharpe, in Chapter 12, finds himself in a blind alleyway with high walls he can't climb and his sword is broken and his rifle is empty and there are 20 Frenchmen staring at him with loaded guns. They say, "Aha! Mr Sharpe, we have got you at last!" and they are right. They have: he's dead. What you have to do at that point is go back to Chapter 3 and put a door in that

174

alleyway. So when they say, "We have you Mr Sharpe," he's able to step through. Now if you did that in Chapter 12, no one would believe you, because they'd think, 'Oh, come on, that door wouldn't be there.' So they do believe you if you establish the door very early in the book. So that's what I do. Obviously it's not literally putting doors in alleyways, but that's more or less what I do, and that's why the first draft takes so long.

I'm sure what drives the book is the character's motivations. The reader knows those motivations, so when he or she has a choice and makes a decision, the reader has to think, 'Yes, that is the decision I would have made in that situation.' So, you have to go back, way back in the book to manipulate things he does or she does, and that's putting that door in the alleyway.

Do you have any other tips for authors or aspiring authors?

I've got lots of tips for aspiring authors. Probably most of them are wrong. You write for yourself, and you write what you want to read. I am very suspicious of writers' groups. I know that a lot of aspiring authors join writers' groups, and I suppose that they think they're going to get encouragement and maybe tips of the trade. But you write for yourself, and writing is a solitary vice. The problem with writers' groups is that so many people take a delight in criticising other people's works to show how clever *they* are.

When I began, I worried about style all the time – style, style, style – and it was totally buggering me up. I was sitting here in America trying to write my first novel, worried about style, and in the end what I did was I took a few pages of a *Hornblower* book and I typed them out so they looked exactly like my manuscript. Then I threw them into a drawer and forgot about what I did and left them there for a few days. Then I reread it in exactly the same way that I was reading my own stuff, and I thought, 'This is terrible! This is awful!' Then I thought, 'Hold on a second, this is a bestselling author,' and that cured it.

Again I'd say this: do not worry about style in the first draft. The first draft is about getting the story right. I think it was John le Carré who said in one of his books, "The first draft is like putting the distemper on the walls, and it's the subsequent rewrites where you make the room look glorious."

BRIAN TRACY

"It's always me and you, one on one … many people write as if they're writing to a stadium full of people."

Brian Tracy is a motivational business guru and bestselling author of 60 books including *Eat That Frog!*, which has sold over five million copies.

He's addressed more than five million people in talks and seminars around the world.

His goal is to help you achieve your personal and business goals faster and more easily than you ever imagined.

I had an interesting experience some years ago: I produced an audio programme and I tried to get it promoted. I found they don't promote audio programmes with newspaper, radio or television interviews, only books. So I wrote it into a book and I sent it out. I used a PR company and I got more than 100 interviews and reviews, and we actually sold 150,000 copies of the book! I said, "This is a really good deal."

Then I found that the news services will not promote a book that's been out for more than 90 days, so I said, "Well, all right, then. I'll write a book every 90 days." This was back in the '90s, and I've actually published 60 books. I'm producing eight this year: six of which are already in the market; the other two will be in the market this fall. My goal was to produce a book every 90 days, and I've done that now consistently for 12 or 13 years.

I developed this system, again because of my time constraints, as I'm on the road continually. The first thing you do is you have to plan out book writing. It's the biggest mistake that authors make: they do it "by-gosh and by-golly" and they do a little bit now and a little bit then and so on. So what I did was I went out and bought a dozen books on "how to write a book" by all the best writers who had spent their lifetimes writing books, and I synthesised their very best recommendations. First of all, is planning your time. So you say a book is going to take 100 hours to write and to polish and to get it ready for publication. (For my first, I spent 300 hours on a book.) You have to plan the amount of time it's going to take.

The second thing I do is what's called a "down dump". I take a legal-size foolscap pad and I start to write down everything I can possibly think that I would put in a book on this subject. For example, I've just come up with a new book, which I'll write this year, and it's going to be called *The Times of Your Life*. What are the times of your life? Well, you talk about creative time, administrative time, learning time, family time, exercise time, personal growth time, then you start to talk about conversation time, meeting time. Every one of these times requires a different focus. For example, work time requires that you focus on high-value tasks and get them done completely. Family time requires that you take lots of unbroken, relaxed, easy time with the most important people in your family, conversing and communicating with them. I've tested these with audiences all over the world and there's a huge need for this book. So that'll be my next subject, *The Times of Your Life* and how you can dramatically increase the quality of your life by realising that time is not the same in every activity. Each activity requires that you use time in a different way. So then I'll write all that down and then I'll break it up into logical chapters. I'll use seven, 12, or 21 chapters. A couple of exceptions, but mostly it's seven or 12 because those are actually cosmic numbers. You'll find it amazing how many books are successful because they have seven or 12 chapters.

I also write what I call "popcorn books", which are books that are loaded with content and they'll have 21 chapters. Sometimes I can cover 21 chapters in 120 pages. I call them the "great ideas" books: there are 21 great ideas for the subject. For example, I wrote a book called *21 Great Ideas to Manage Your Time and Double Your Productivity* and the book came out as *Eat That Frog!* and it sold five million copies. We changed the title and the catch-line, and that book is now one of the bestselling books on time management in the history of man on earth, and it was basically 21 key bullet points on the subject. I also did *21 Great Ways to Live to Be 100* and *21 Great Ways to Build a High Profit Business*. That becomes my model – seven,

12 or 21 – depending upon the nature of the subject. Then I will write an outline of the book and what each chapter will contain. Then I'll run it up the flagpole of several publishers who've published me before, and I'll say, "I'm thinking of writing a book on this subject, are you interested?" With almost no exceptions, one or more publishers will come back and say, "We like that book; that will fit into our line for next spring," or "That would be a good book; we would be very interested in that." We will then negotiate an advance and what I call a "drop-dead date", the date that they will have to have the book in their hands in order to publish it at a specific time.

I also require two things. First of all, we have an agreement on *when* the book comes out, because I'm writing four books a year and I don't like them to come out on top of each other, and neither do the publishers. I just did a book last year called *The Power of Self-Confidence*. They asked me at John Wiley, the sixth biggest publishing company in the world, "Would you write a book for us on self-confidence?" and I said, "Yes, but we have to agree upon a date." So they said, "We will bring it out in September, if you can promise us not to bring a book out for three months prior or three months afterwards." I just happened to have that window and I said, "Great." So they sent me a contract and an advance, and I sent them a book back on the drop-dead date. The book was released in September, and it's now worldwide in multiple languages. So that's my approach to writing books.

Once I have the drop-dead date, then I sit down and start to get really tight with the schedule. How many hours is it going to take me to write this book – first of all, to assemble all the information? Usually, I have all the information in my mind. I write 200 and 300-page books out of my mental storehouse, because I read for about three

180

hours a day. I'm giving you a lot of information, but one of the things I learned from the very beginning, is if you're not a voracious reader, forget about being a writer. You've got to read and read and read and read. You've got to constantly be reading in order to keep building up your mental storehouse of words, pictures, ideas, images and concepts.

If I'm going to write a book on time management, I'll read ten books on time management, attend six time management seminars, buy ten time management programmes, and listen to half a dozen time management audios. I'll spend a year or two years just drowning in time management concepts, and then I just synthesise them in a whole different way. So you have to be a reader if you want to be a writer. That's not just my concept: that goes back to Steinbeck and Hemingway and other Nobel Prize winners.

Anyway, once I get it all laid out, then what I do is I dictate the entire book from cover to cover. Then I send it on to my secretary who then types it all out and sends it back to me. Then, I start to work. I go through the manuscript five times: word for word, comma for comma, letter for letter – from beginning to end. I clean it up, tighten it up, polish it, and move stuff around, until I finally reach the point where I don't think I can improve it any more. This is another secret to success in writing: you keep rewriting until you're completely happy with it. You just cannot think of how you could improve it. You've done it four or five times and it has a nice flow to it.

If you're writing non-fiction, it's very important that you think of this. My best definition for non-fiction comes from Ralph Waldo Emerson, where he said, "It is an enthusiastic conversation on paper." You'll find most bestselling books are "an enthusiastic conversation on paper". The person is talking to one person who they really like and care about, and who they are really excited about sharing this information with, and they're talking in a very positive, happy, healthy way to someone who they like and respect. So I always use the word "you": *When you do this and you've probably had this experience. When you learn how to do this, you will get this kind of a result.* Then, I flip it back to myself: *When I first learned this concept, I was struggling in this area, but once I began to apply it, I got these huge results.* It's always *me* and *you*, one on one. I say that because many people write as if they're writing to a stadium full of people, not anybody in particular. So one of the things that I learned very early in my craft is to think about somebody you really care about: your spouse, your child or your best friend; someone you went to college with, a co-worker. Think about that person. Mentally put a little statue of that person in front of you when you're writing and talk to that one person, and it'll come out. If it reads well to one person, it will read well to a lot of people.

What about promotion of your books once they come out? What sort of things have you found to be the most effective at boosting your book sales, either online or offline?

This is becoming one of the most challenging of all areas. The first thing is, if you self-publish you're going to have to sell the book by yourself, one-on-one, and make a nickel a book. So the idea of self-publishing is something that I've never done. I've only done it when I've had a client who's promised to buy 50,000 copies and then I'll publish myself and not go through a publisher. But 95 to 98 percent of my books, I publish with publishers. Even though I'll receive a lower royalty, they'll put the book in every store in the country, if not worldwide. That's the benefit of working with a publisher. Here's two points: if the publisher won't accept a book, then something needs to be improved in the book. Second of all, if it's not published by a publisher, nobody will interview you or promote you on the book. Any self-published books are immediately thrown in the wastebasket when they get to any kind of book reviewers. Radio, newspaper, magazines, television won't even consider them. So therefore the key is to get someone who really likes the book concept enough to say they'll publish it. They'll put their money on the table as well.

I've worked with everything from very large advances to no advances at all. My book called *Eat That Frog!* is with a publisher that does not give advances, but they give very high royalties and they're very impressive about promotion. So they send me a lot of money every year in royalties. They say they've paid me more royalties than any other author in their history. It's probably pushing two million dollars now, although they don't pay advances. That's the trade-off.

Authors can say, "I want to get a big advance." The advance is for most authors – 80 to 90 percent of authors – the only money they will ever receive. Because the book won't ever earn back the advance just because of the economics of the book industry. So a lot of people out there are saying, "Get the maximum advance, don't go with these people." If you're a new author, you have to go hat in hand. You have to darn near beg them to take your book and give you a pittance as an advance. Once you're an established author, publishers are just like any business person; they sell more of whatever sells off the shelves. If your book sells, they'll publish more of your books. If they don't, they'll stop. So, do anything to get a real, live publisher.

Publishers then have agents; publishing agents who actually go and call on every book vendor in the country and act as agents for all of the publishers. They'll call on every person who has the ability to put your book in a bookstore in the country to introduce your book to them. You cannot do that by yourself, so that's why you want to use a publisher. There are all kinds of people who say, "I'm going straight to e-book." The only people who are going straight to e-book and selling anything today are extremely well-known authors. Seth Godin, the author on marketing, says, "I'll only do e-book from now on." Well, he's already sold several million copies, and he's got a huge database, so it's very easy for people seeking him out to find a book.

The other thing about self-publishing is, you're going to have to do 75 percent – maybe 80, maybe 90 percent – of the work yourself. Book publishers always have a love-hate relationship with their authors: if they publish the book they'll run it up a few flagpoles, they'll announce it to a few publications in the industry, maybe send out copies to some of the major bookstore chains, and then they'll wait. If no orders come in, they forget about it and move on to the next book. So what you have to do is hire a professional PR person (and most of them are dreadful, so you're always gambling, and they still charge you the same amount). They don't just do 50 calls a day. That person's job is to phone up – they call it the "phone-and-bug method" – and bug publications or reviewers to take the book and review it. They just phone-and-bug, phone-and-bug, phone-and-bug; and then follow up phone-and-bug.

My friend Ken Blanchard paired up with Spencer Johnson to write a book called *The One-Minute Manager*. He started a consulting company out here in San Diego. They went out and dutifully did phone calls and radio, and still couldn't sell the book. Well, Ken was doing a talk for the Young Presidents' Organization, which is made up of presidents of multi-million dollar companies under the age of 45, and he's got a wonderful personality. He did this really genial little talk for them at a low price, and one of them said, "I've got a friend who has a morning news show in Minneapolis, and I could get him to review your book." So he went on the show, he's a very charming guy, they loved the interview, and it was picked up from a New York station by *Good Morning America*. They interviewed him and the book went ballistic and became one of the bestselling books in history. That was the sort of thing that is like getting lightning to strike, it's so rare. He just kept pounding month after month.

My friends, Jack Canfield and Mark Victor Hansen, who published the *Chicken Soup for the Soul* series, published the books and the books just sat there, month after month. Every day they came in and they did three promotional activities. They physically went down to the local newspaper, they called the radio shows, they appeared with their books in shopping centres, and they went to book shows. They did three things a day for six months, and suddenly the book hit. One good review in the *Los Angeles Times* caused people all over Los Angeles to storm the bookstores and say, "Where's the book?" They bought the book, and when they bought the book, people began to send copies around, and they sold 100 million copies of *the Chicken Soup for the Soul* series.

So what I'm saying is there's no consistent way of doing it, but you have to be responsible. You must be prepared to put your head down for at least six months or more. I have friends who have promoted their books for two or three years; that's all they did. They got up in the morning, they did their day job, and then in the evenings and weekends, all they did was promote the book and the book still never sold. There's a wonderful one-liner I learned when I was doing my studies about writing books that goes, "There are three keys to writing a bestselling book, and nobody knows what they are." If ever an author asks how they get their book to be a bestseller, that's what I tell them.

In your experience, is online or offline book marketing more effective? Many authors I talk to are saying that online marketing is a quicker and faster way than doing traditional things like signings and talks.

I think so. I refuse to do interviews, other than interviews like this. I won't do TV interviews, I'll only do telephone interviews. Why is that? It's because it's massively time-consuming. It's incredibly expensive. I've flown across the country to be on a New York morning show for six minutes, and how much leverage do you get from that? Very, very little. So online is better and better.

As you know from the stories of people who have been online hits, there's a sort of formula: you have to go on chat shows, you have to review your book, you have to recommend it, you have to form blogs, you have to go on other people's chats, and so on. Some people work for months and months and months until people start to buy their book. Other people can work for months and months and months and no one will buy their damn book. So there are a whole lot of online strategies. One of them is to offer the first chapter free, or even two chapters for free. Go to every single website you can think of that has anybody that would be interested in the book and offer it for free, and hope that your friends will viral the book.

You can also publish it, as I have done – one book, just to say I had done it – I published with Amazon as an e-book. It's called *Close That Sale!* Now my programme, *The Art of Closing the Sale* and my book, *The Art of Closing the Sale* have sold hundreds of thousands, millions of dollars' worth. On Amazon as an e-book – same book, same author, same content – almost no uptake at all. Why is that? When I began writing, the US publishers were publishing about 225,000 books a year – that was back in 1979. (I do a lot of research by the way, that's another thing. If you want to be a successful author you've got to keep current with what's going on in the book industry.) Last year, the major publishers in the US published about 220,000 books. It hasn't changed in 30 years. So what happened?

Well, what happened is, last year they published three million books (in English), and this year they published four million, next year five million. All those are self-published and e-books. As soon as somebody made a couple of dollars or pounds, producing an e-book and marketing it, every would-be author in the world decided to write and publish an e-book, and the market is just literally drowned. There's an ocean of e-books out there. The sweet spot for an e-book is about 99 cents. You can actually take it up to about $2.99 before the sales will stop. Unless, of course, it's published by a major publisher, in which case they'll pay for 50 percent of cost of what a hardcover would be. But for e-books it's between 99 cents and $2.99, and you'd be absolutely astonished, if you've done your homework, at how many people have worked their hearts out to publish a book for free just to get *anybody* to read it or comment on it. They're just desperate for readership. So that's one way to do it. You can write a book and publish it as an e-book for nothing. You just pay a percentage of the sales price to Amazon or to other companies that will carry it.

You've spoken to over five million people in 62 countries around the world. What are your top tips for authors to help them get the most out of speaking in front of large audiences?

Well, first, second and third thing is: be a great speaker, be a great speaker, be a great speaker. Be a really excellent speaker, which is a whole other thing. Most authors who are only authors, are absolutely dreadful speakers. You just cringe when you listen to them, because they do no preparation and they simply read pieces of their book, and maybe *one* person in the audience will buy the book. So you start to think about: how much am I earning per hour to sell books by speaking?

If you're a well-known author and an excellent speaker, well then they'll buy *piles* of your books! I never do it because there's too much trouble in trucking the boxes, laying them out, hiring staff to sell them, take the credit cards, some of which bounce, cheques which afterwards bounce, and it's not that easy to get a speaking engagement where they will allow you to get up there and sell your book. What I use is what I call "the law of indirect effort." If you speak really well on your subject, so that people really like it and enjoy it, people are hungry for more, then they'll say, "Have you got a book on this?" or they'll find the book themselves.

The other thing is that they won't buy the book at your public function. Why is that? It's because of the phenomenon called "showrooming". Showrooming is now becoming a major, major world economic problem. People go to major stores shopping, like Walmart or Marks & Spencer or wherever it happens to be, and they'll find something that they like and they'll put it on their camera. They'll take a photograph of the barcode on the product and just punch it in. In seconds, the lowest possible price and location and availability of that book in the United Kingdom or United States or whatever country you're in will come back. So what they do is they showroom. They go to see the product they like, then they'll take photographs of the barcode, and go and order them online for 30 percent off. So Amazon, for example, sells all their books at 30 percent off. So if I want to sell a book – and I sell thousands of books a year just because people order them through my website – I have to offer it for 30 percent off.

When I publish a book, I always negotiate purchase rights with the publisher. I always say that I must be able to buy the book myself for 25 percent of retail. If I can't buy it myself at that price, then I won't promote it. We go back and forth and back and forth. Most of my publishers will give me the books at 25 to 30 percent of retail, then I can buy them and I can mark them up to 70 percent of retail, the Amazon price, and I can make a profit. One of the first things publishers try to say is, "This is our standard contract. Every single author in the world has signed this contract. We never deviate from this contract. We never reduce the price of books to our authors to more than 50 or 60 percent off," but if you were a bookstore, you could buy 50, 60 and 65 percent off retail. Then they want you to buy 500-1,000 copies to give you a discount, which you may have no ability to sell because you're too small.

This negotiation I learned from professional writers before I began my career: pre-negotiate a reduced rate at which you can buy your own books from the publisher. Everything that you buy from them is 100 percent profit for them anyway. In many cases, they try to actually earn back their advance or make a bit of profit by selling you books at such a high price that there's no room in it for you to sell them yourself. If you're paying 50 percent of retail to your publisher – which is what is in most publishing contracts – you have to lower the price 30 percent to compete with Amazon, or people will actually sit in your audience with their iPhones and they will order the book from Amazon online while you're talking. Then you'll find your books gathering dust at the back of the room, even though you gave a great talk! This is what happens. They're sitting there, and it just takes two seconds to find the cheapest version of your book available anywhere in the world, including shipping and handling, and it'll be there in two or three days. Amazon now delivers overnight – it's unbelievable. It used to be five to seven days if you ordered a book. Now you hardly have time to clear your mental calendar to read the book before it's there. So this is what you're going up against.

One of the things you can do if you're a good speaker is you can pre-sell books. It's another strategy: you say, "Look, what do you want to send your people away with? Well, I'll sell you my books at discount, and you can buy a copy for everyone in your audience." Many speakers earn as much or more from sales of their books to everyone in their audience pre-purchased by their client – not sold one by one – and earn more that way. They'll have a captive audience, but they'll still have to match the Amazon price because as soon as you quote a price to your speaking client, they showroom you. They'll immediately go on to Google and type the title of your book and "cheapest price", and they'll find the cheapest price in the world from people who sell your books in quantity. So anyway, it's a challenge.

The critical thing about success as an author is: number one, write a good book; number two, write a good book; number three, write a good book. If you do those three, then people will pass your book on. It's called "pass-along", and you'll sell by word of mouth. People will start to hear about the book and recommend the book. Almost every book that I buy – you can see my den, I'm just surrounded by thousands of books, I consume them copiously – it's because someone said, "It's a good book." They say, "Did you read this book? It's a good book," and sitting there at my table I just go on Amazon – ping, ping, ping – and order it, and it's in my house the next day. So 85 percent of your book sales will come from word of mouth.

The key is write a good book, and tell everybody what a good book it is, and get people to read it and comment on it. That's how you sort of get the ice floe moving. You've got to break up the natural resistance to the fact that people are overwhelmed with so many books and simultaneously people have less and less time to read them. You're going up against that.

You use Facebook, YouTube and Twitter. Do you have any strategies that work particularly effectively with social media when promoting books or keeping in touch with readers?

The most important word in your life or my life or in the life of a business is *credibility* – to have people believe you and believe in you. People who follow you on Facebook or Twitter or LinkedIn or something else are people who like you and believe in you. I have a team of four people who do social media strategy in conjunction with everything else that I offer. (I offer a lot of other products in addition to books.) What they will do is build up my Twitter followers to 145,000, Facebook 100,000, LinkedIn, thousands of people, and they send out messages every single day. It could be quotes, updates, news, or my background. It could be pictures from my family vacation. It could be a video from me talking about what Easter means to people throughout the Western world. They're constantly thinking, 'What we can do that would get that thumbs-up?' or what they call a 'like' on Facebook. Or, 'What could we do that would be viral, that people who liked it would pass on to someone else?' So we work on every single thing we can do.

First of all, if you want a social media strategy, buy the books on the subject and read them. If you want to do an e-book, there are eight or nine books on how to write and publish successful e-books that are on Amazon e-books, and most of them are free. What you do is you immerse yourself in the craft and learn exactly what you have to write in an e-book to get people to download it, even if it's free.

The issue today is not money; it's time. A person is not going to download the book unless they feel it will justify the time that will be necessary to read it. So they'll tell you to write an e-book and make it punchy. I call it a "Cracker Jack book", like the snacks: people can read little bits of it and get something out of it. Some people call them a toilet book (it's a terrible name, but everybody knows what that means), something that you can read in short pieces and still get something of value. Then you have to settle down and you have to develop a five-year social media strategy. You can't just send out something once a week or once a month. You have to be really serious about it.

Acknowledgements

Every day, I wake up and thank my lucky stars for all the wonderful people in my life: my family, my friends, my mentors, my clients, my business partners, and the people I hear from on a daily basis who have signed up to my various newsletters.

Every one of you has made a contribution to this book in different ways, both big and small. It may be with a smile here, a thought-provoking question, an encouraging word or guidance there.

There are so many people to thank – friends who have generously given their time and advice – that I really don't know where to begin.

A mentor's guidance lasts not just for a few years but for a lifetime – as does my gratitude. So a huge thank you will always go to Mark Anastasi, who taught me to think so much bigger than I ever thought possible. Also to Lee McIntyre, who generously shared his wisdom and experience, and gave me encouragement whenever I hit a 'wall'.

Thanks also to my publishing mentor, Steve Harrison, at Bradley Communications, who gently pointed out my shortcomings and nudged me in the right direction. Also to Jack Canfield and Dan Kennedy for their great marketing ideas.

Thanks to Greg Secker, Matt Shaw, Guy Cohen, Vince Stanzione, Ian Williams, Allan Kingdon and Noel Mason. Their encouragement and inspiration helped a technophobic and mathematically-challenged woman with self-doubts to believe 'I can do it.' Thanks to Greg, Matt and Guy in particular for the opportunities you gave me.

Thanks to Leili McKinley, Ciaran Doyle and Gareth Owen for their Internet marketing and social media expertise and for sharing this so generously. Thanks to Rosarie Nolan, Geoffrey Berwind and Joanna Martin for helping refine my public speaking skills.

Huge thanks go to the team who have helped to make this book possible: Paddy McAllister for web development; Barbara Doherty for stunning cover design; Colette de Colbert for diligent typesetting; Matt and Diana Horner for e-book and Kindle expertise; Krista Ehasz for transcription; Elizabeth Baker for proofreading; Anna Swan for fastidious editing; Ella Gascoigne for superb PR. It has been a real team effort. All of you have helped with an energy and enthusiasm that has been humbling.

Thanks to my Mum and Dad for your support and love. You taught me the importance of the proverb: "When the wind of change blows, some build walls and others build windmills." I've experienced a few hurricanes over the years, but you've given me the strength to turn negatives into positives.

Thanks also to my grandparents, long departed now, for helping to shape me into the person I am today. We miss you, but your echoes will always be with us.

Thanks to my sister, Chloe, for artistic flair: for playing around with colours and fonts, until we got the right branding.

Thank you to my partner, Chris, for making me laugh at all times of day and night, and for being the kindest person anyone could wish to share their life with.

Thanks also to my children – Cormac, Tierni and Chiara – for warm hugs, beautiful smiles, great fun and laughter.
I love you and couldn't have done a page of this without you.

The Author's Vault

FREE Training and Bonuses:

- *How to Find a Publisher or Literary Agent.*
- *How to Avoid Your Book Ending Up on the Publishing Slush Pile.*
- *How to Choose a Bestselling Book Title.*
- *Mistakes to Avoid with Agents and Publishers.*
- *Red Flags to Watch Out for in Your Publishing Contract.*
- *How to Write a Marketing Plan for Your Book.*
- *Can I Quote Someone Else in My Book Without Permission?*
- *Should I Use 'Fifty Shades of X' as a Book Title?*
- *How to Write Your Book Faster.*
- *How to Choose the Best Cover for Your E-Book or Kindle Book.*
- *Should I Self-Publish or is a Mainstream Publisher Better?*
- *How to Get Your Book into Airport Bookshops.*
- *How to Stop Other Authors Stealing Your Book or Film Idea.*
- *Should I Disguise Real-Life Characters in My Book?*
- *How to Get Celebrity Endorsements for Your Book.*
- *What Do Publishers' Rejection Letters really Mean?*
- *And much, much more.*

Get your FREE reports now at:
www.CelebrityAuthorsSecrets.com/Vault

Author Mentoring

Stephanie J. Hale works with: TV and film celebrities; Hollywood scriptwriters; millionaire authors; bestselling authors; members of the Royal household; and the world's most famous entrepreneurs and thought leaders.

She also loves working with novice authors who are writing books for the first time, helping them turn their books into bestsellers. She's helped several authors achieve £1million+ a year with self-publishing and e-books.

For more help with writing, publishing or selling your book, go to:

www.CelebrityAuthorsSecrets.com

If you like this book, please give it a 5-star review on Amazon.

Lightning Source UK Ltd.
Milton Keynes UK
UKOW03f0806200314

228496UK00001B/9/P